PENGUIN BOO

THE MEDIEVAL C

Philip Warner, a native c
since 1600 and a graduate
mainly on military histc
required extensive travel a

He served in the army thr
Far East, and was subsequently an Assistant Principal at the War Office,
working in the Defence Materials Division, a Lecturer for the British
Council in Spain, and a Senior Lecturer and Head of Communication
Studies at the Royal M   He was a military
obituaries corresponder   . He was a
member of the Royal Archaeological Institute. When not researching or
writing, his recreations included rugby football, fly-fishing, sociable
wine-drinking, conversation and music of all varieties, and he was a
member of the Athenaeum, the Harlequin Rugby Club, Jesters' Squash
Club and Sandhurst's trout-fishing club.

Philip Warner died in September 2000. In its obituary, the *Daily Telegraph*
described him as 'an outstanding military historian' and 'a master of the
laconic, lapidary phrase'.

D0920257

Frontispiece: The Castle of Saumur at harvest time. The elegant
magnificence of this castle reflects the pride which the Duke of Berry
took in his possessions. This one was built in the late fourteenth
century. Note the vineyards approaching close to the walls, and the
kitchen to the left away from the main building. Although more of a
residence than a fortress, there is no doubt that this castle could have
put up a strong resistance. The base of the towers is very strong, the
drawbridge protects a very narrow gateway, iron grilles cover the
lower windows, and there is a wealth of machicolation. The conical
roofs would deflect missiles. Note the tilt (p. 97) by the railings

THE MEDIEVAL CASTLE

Life in a fortress in peace and war

Philip Warner

PENGUIN BOOKS

PENGUIN BOOKS

Published by the Penguin Group
Penguin Books Ltd, 80 Strand, London WC2R 0RL, England
Penguin Putnam Inc., 375 Hudson Street, New York, New York 10014, USA
Penguin Books Australia Ltd, Ringwood, Victoria, Australia
Penguin Books Canada Ltd, 10 Alcorn Avenue, Toronto, Ontario, Canada M4V 3B2
Penguin Books India (P) Ltd, 11 Community Centre, Panchsheel Park,
New Delhi – 110 017, India
Penguin Books (NZ) Ltd, Cnr Rosedale and Airborne Roads, Albany, Auckland,
New Zealand
Penguin Books (South Africa) (Pty) Ltd, 24 Sturdee Avenue, Rosebank 2196, South Africa

Penguin Books Ltd, Registered Offices: 80 Strand, London WC2R 0RL, England

www.penguin.com

First published by Weidenfeld & Nicolson 1971
Published as a Classic Penguin 2001
2

Printed in England by Cox & Wyman Ltd, Reading, Berkshire

Contents

Illustrations

Preface

One of the pleasantest privileges of an author is to be able to use his preface to thank all the helpful people who have refused to be thanked in any other way. On this occasion they cannot wave away one's gratitude and adroitly change the subject; the thanks go down in black and white.

There is Brigadier Peter Young, DSO, MC, MA, who gave me every encouragement and help to write this book; W.L. McElwee, Esq., MC, MA, who gave me much useful advice; T.D. Tremlett, Esq., MA, FSA, and R. Luckett, Esq., BA, whose encouraging suggestions saved me hours of time; and Major D.N. Hopkins, MBE, with whom I have had much valuable discussion.

My daughter Diana has meticulously checked every sentence; my sons, Richard and John, have had to translate obscure texts and check references. All three have stood on windswept crags and pretended to enjoy the experience while I was pondering at excessive length on what men might have thought a thousand years ago.

Lt. Col. Ririd Myddleton, MVO, TD, DL, JP, sent me much valuable information about Chirk Castle; Major Charles Chenevix-Trench, MC, kindly allowed me to use references from his fascinating book *The Poacher and the Squire*; J.J. Bagley, Esq., kindly allowed me to quote from *Life in Medieval England,* and Messrs Faber and Faber, Oxford

University Press, Methuen, and Her Majesty's Stationery Office gave permission to quote extracts from their publications.

I am particularly grateful to Mrs Philippa Booth who took enormous trouble over diagrams and illustrations.

There are many other people whose help and encouragement has been of great value: old friends such as Brigadier T.R.Henn, CBE, of St Catharine's College, Cambridge, Lt.-Col. G.A.Shepperd, MBE, and J.W.Taylor, Esq., OBE of the Central Library at the RMA Sandhurst, the patient and helpful library staff both at Sandhurst and the Camberley Public Library, the Society of Antiquaries – my debts are without limit.

Finally, Mrs Freda Marsh who can not only read my writing but even seems to like doing so. I sent her pages of indecipherable scrawl and received in return pages of beautiful typescript.

To them all, I owe a debt of gratitude. I shall never be able to repay it because, even if I could, they would not let me do so.

Introduction

In this book we trace the story of the medieval castle from its beginnings to the height of its influence. The need for this type of fortification began when the Roman Empire broke up, but many years were to elapse before castles were developed. During the intervening period there were migrations of people into and around the area which is now called Europe, and from these movements the character of Europe as a whole, and of its constituent parts, was formed. Subsequent events, such as the Norman conquest of England, dynastic marriages, wars, and economic development, changed some of the details, but the matrix remained un-altered. The principal stabilizing factor in the Middle Ages was the castle, but in order to understand what it accomplished it is necessary to know something of the political and historical background, the origins of some of the castle builders, and the characteristics of the areas in which castles were built. This information, and the military theory which went with it, is kept to a minimum, but the reader will realise that much more might be said were there space enough; and, as in all military matters, there is no adequate substitute for a personal survey of the ground; 'time spent in reconnaissance is seldom wasted'.

The influence of castles on the course of history seems to have been greatly underrated. In the early part of this book we discuss what castles could and did accomplish. From that we proceed to a survey of the conditions which brought them into being. This is followed by an account of the factors which caused them to be developed and modified. Weapons, training, and methods of castle warfare then come under review. The castle was not only a fortress, it was a home, so recreation, food, and custom, are also surveyed. Where possible, comparisons are made with fortress and barrack life in other periods, particularly the present day, as this may help towards a clearer understanding of both the medieval mind and the essential sameness of military requirements – courage, stamina, resourcefulness and determination – to say nothing of the peculiar psychological problems which can arise in any military situation at any time.

In tracing the evolution of techniques of fortification we are also following the emergence of modern Europe. First one area, then another, had a commanding influence. The Normans were able to enforce their feudal organization because they had a technique of rapid castle-building. The Middle East later exercised its influence through the Crusades; this was exerted gradually over three hundred years. Italian crossbowmen were once thought to be the masters of warfare, but in the fourteenth century they were cut to pieces by the longbow, which originated in Wales. The most successful fortresses were those which adapted the best features of every phase, and consequently we find the later castles with loops for longbow fire, croslets to accommodate crossbows, and gunloops for artillery; this, of course, is only one aspect of their versatility.

Castles were sited and built to meet a military requirement. The requirement would have been previously assessed by making a military appreciation of the situation. The essential of a successful military appreciation is that no factor which might influence a campaign should be omitted or unassessed. Many of these factors are obvious, e.g. the relative strength of armies, the ground, morale on each side, timing, the courses open to one's own troops, the courses open to enemy troops, and the possibility of prolonged resistance. Other factors might be impossible to assess with any degree of certainty; among them would be such matters as whether traditional enemies could be trusted to fight side by side in one's own army.

When Edward I of England built a chain of extremely expensive castles in north Wales he might have seemed to his contemporaries to be over-insuring against further insurrection in that area. Such criticisms are hard to refute because nobody knows whether lesser fortifications might have had an adequate deterrent effect. It seems however that Edward, who had many calls on his finances, was unlikely to have over-estimated the requirement. He was an extremely able soldier, of great and varied experience, and he made considerable use of women spies. He was unlikely to have omitted any factor in his appreciation.

In considering castles it is not only interesting and useful but also essential to apply the technique of the military appreciation to the castle-builder's situation. It may involve one in a study of ethnic groupings, of weather conditions, of trade, or similar matters, but it is only by a comprehensive survey that one can understand why, where, and how medieval castles were built.

Castle holders were usually either kings or powerful barons. Kings and barons travelled extensively. They campaigned abroad, and they also moved frequently from one castle to another. Some spent more time abroad than they spent in their homelands, and all aristocrats had more in common with their foreign counterparts than with their own inferiors at home. In consequence, military, social, and cultural ideas were exchanged between different countries. Thus the towers and barbican at Warwick castle, built by the Beauchamps in the fourteenth century, are more French in style than English.

A study of life in medieval castles shows a rigid social structure. Aristocrats might encounter opposition from their social equals but rarely from inferiors. Many of the top administrative posts in castles became as hereditary as titles, and their holders, butlers, chancellors, marshalls, took their names from their posts. The lower classes also took their names from their jobs, but while the surname became hereditary the job sometimes changed. This produced a peculiar situation by which one man might have several names. Nevertheless, names often provide a valuable guide to the structure of medieval life. In this fighting man's world it was inevitable that much time and thought would be given to weapons, training, and mock warfare, the design and care of armour, experiments with siege engines, plans, and endless impracticable schemes.

For the privileged and powerful the life of the medieval soldier was rich and full-blooded: men pressed their luck to the limit. Moderation was observed only when there was no possible alternative; otherwise feasting, fighting, loving, drinking, gambling, and campaigning continued until utter exhaustion put an end to them. When the inevitable reckoning had to be met, men sought a swift death in battle or even tried to escape the consequences of a lifetime of excess by retiring to the austere life and diet of a monastery.

Many readers ignore appendices, which they suspect will be full of obscure and pettifogging detail. In this book the appendices have been used for information which is essential and interesting but a little too detailed for the main text.

I

Why Castles
were Evolved

The primary function of the medieval castle was to dominate. It was not, as is commonly believed, a refuge in which men cowered behind walls. There were indeed occasions when men were forced to defend themselves behind cover, but the object of building a castle was not to retreat from conflict but to control it. The appearance of a castle is misleading. The moat, drawbridge, portcullis, and arrow-loops give the impression that the castle functioned within bowshot range only. On the contrary it influenced an area of at least twenty-five miles' radius. Even a footsoldier could cover thirty miles in a day without difficulty, and the horseman could obviously manage more. Medieval soldiers did not sit at home in the barracks twiddling their thumbs. They were out patrolling, looking for trouble and frequently making it.

The great days of the medieval castle were between the years 900 and 1500. Before the earlier date there were strong fortifications, walled towns, and substantial earthworks, but the castle did not exist in its medieval form. In six hundred years the castle evolved from an earth and wood construction to a highly sophisticated stone building which incorporated all the military lore which had been accumulated throughout what is called, for want of a better word, civilization. It had everything from dungeons in which prisoners could be interrogated under torture to machicolations through which quicklime and incendiary missiles could be directed on to the attacker.

The commander, who was called the castellan, was usually a man of considerable and varied qualities. His accomplishments had to include much more than the military skill to direct a dogged last stand. In addition he had to administer an area, and possess what is now called 'top management ability'. Not least of his problems was that of stores. For long periods castles enjoyed a peaceful existence and danger would seem remote. But suddenly the situation could change. The first warning would be terrified peasants from outlying areas who had lost what little property they possessed, and been lucky to escape with their lives. Immediate decisions would have to be made. Was this a raid which would soon exhaust itself or might be beaten off with a small expeditionary force, or was it something much bigger? If the latter, the district must be put into a state of defence. Peasants, cattle, stores, weapons and food must all be brought into the castle. Engines must be positioned, and woe betide those responsible if the ammunition supplies had been allowed to run down. The expenditure of missiles was prodigious. At Kenilworth in 1266 the volleys of stones from catapult and sling were so fierce and continuous that projectiles were constantly colliding in mid-air. Admittedly they were attacking on a narrow front, but even so the concentration and volume of fire were remarkable. Nor was Kenilworth the only besieged castle to experience this intensity of fire and counter-fire.

The widespread belief that in peacetime a castle was merely

the stage for courtly love, stately banquets, and considerable boredom, is very wide of the mark. Today's peaceful scene of deserted rooms and attractive gardens would have been divided between commissariat, ordnance factory, barrack square and proving ground. It would have been at least as noisy as a modern factory; communication would be by shouting, and men who were not hammering would probably be chopping. The ubiquitous smith would be shoeing horses or repairing armour and weapons; his contribution to the general clatter would be particularly noticeable, and there would be plenty of smiths. Even a monastery would have been a busy noisy place, but a castle must at times have been almost intolerable.

The medieval castle had certain features which distinguished it from previous fortifications. It was personal. It belonged to the king or to a baron. It was not held by the community as a town was, and when it afforded refuge it did so on its own terms. In its early, though not in its later, stages it was economical to build and maintain. Labour was cheap and plentiful; much of the time it was not only plentiful but free. Later in the Middle Ages the cost of work rose sharply but this was because of the shortage caused by plague and the need for skilled craftsmen. The earliest castles could be, and were, erected by unskilled or semi-skilled workmen. In the French motte and bailey form they could have been built a thousand years earlier, and if they had existed might have made a considerable difference to the course of history. The motte and bailey castle, to be described in greater detail later, was a mound of earth with a ditch at the bottom and a palisade around the top. Within the palisade there would probably, but not invariably, be a wooden tower. In fact, if Neolithic man had had any use for a motte and bailey castle he could probably have built one.

The castle system became useful when populations became settled, but conquerors were still likely to be on the move. Although, as we have noted earlier, castles were not designed as refuges, they were magnificent devices for delaying and dislocating an invading army. Their importance in this is easily explained.

When an army, even a modern army, sets off it is promptly confronted with communication problems. If it advances on a wide front it will be lucky if the flanks and the centre are not soon straying from the position the commander would like them to occupy. It was so with the Battle of Bouvines in 1214, with the great Schlieffen Plan in 1914, and it occurred again in the Ardennes in 1944 – to quote but a few of the many examples available. A flooded stream, a broken bridge or even a misread map can cause havoc. Even apparently trivial obstacles such as hillocks, hedgerows or patches of marshy ground can alter an entire battle plan. It was therefore the aim of the castle strategist to place his fortification at a point where it would either enhance a natural obstacle or create an entirely fresh one in its own right. Ideally it would be placed where it would command one or more valleys, be an excellent observation post, and be extremely difficult to capture. However, there were special liabilities involved in siting castles in lofty places, and these had to be guarded against. When a castle was situated in mountainous country there might be difficulty in feeding its garrison and thus, in a siege, it could easily be starved into surrender. Under certain circumstances, a very light siege maintained over a period would suffice to bring out a starving garrison. Another liability would be the one which garrisons still face today: lonely, boring, inaccessible places are bad for morale. They tend to be regarded by their occupants as punishment stations or their equivalent. Yet another drawback is that they are difficult to relieve. When Château Gaillard, near Rouen, was besieged by Philip Augustus of France in 1203, a combined land and river operation was mounted to free it. But the fact that the besiegers had already occupied the space between the castle and the river gave them as big an advantage over the relievers as the castle-holders themselves enjoyed over the besieging force. In theory the French should have been caught in a pincer between a sally from the garrison and the advancing relief, but the swift river current and rough terrain soon disposed of theory.

Many of the most important castles were built on flat or even hollow ground, and these were frequently the most formidable. Their protection was marsh and water. It was unusual for them to have to stand sieges. An invader looking at them would decide that the project was impossible. When William the Conqueror crossed from Normandy to England in 1066 he took powerful continental supporters. One of them was William de Braose, who was rewarded with extensive lands in the south of England. Braose established a castle a few miles from Shoreham in Sussex and it preserves its essential characteristics today. Nearly all the masonry has gone but the small portion which remains is a great tribute to the tenacity of medieval cement. The castle itself was on a tall mound surrounded by a moat which, formerly, was filled by tidal water. The environment is fairly flat but the mound itself is natural, though doubtless its sides were cut to increase its steepness. It is a revealing experience to climb that mound from the dry moat. There are plenty of scrubby branches to hold on to and the sides are not unduly slippery, but the thought of crossing a tidal moat and then crawling up the steep, bare mound, down which stones, arrows and darts would be hurled, is challenging. But such deeds were done when necessity dictated.

The reason why all castles appear to have been built in picturesque and remote situations is that they have survived more successfully under those conditions. Castles built near fords, in towns or on crossing-places have often been demolished for convenience, for the sake of their building material, or because they had become insanitary or unsafe. When they occupied sites of strategic or tactical value, they were usually replaced by modern counterparts or perhaps flattened to clear a field of fire. Only recently have attempts been made to preserve castles of great historical interest, and even today we still hear the sad news that a building which could well have been incorporated in a community rec-reational area has been demolished to create characterless suburbia that could, with equal convenience, have been sited elsewhere.

It is natural that in the course of thousands of years of tribal and district warfare practically every point of strategic or tactical importance would have been noted, partly fortified, and probably used. Thus, all over Europe there are traces of defensive ditches, embankments or ambushes. Nevertheless, they belong to a different defensive concept from the castle. They would be made and occupied by a tribe and the object of their construction was to check and destroy an invader. They represented a simple tactical device to make the oncomer fight at a disadvantage. If we accept the hypo-thesis that one man behind a defence is worth three in attack, the old earthworks must have made the path of the aggressor difficult. However, they were not nearly as effective as castles, for reasons which we shall see later.

Castle strategy belongs to a larger concept of warfare. Castles were not only sited on fords, at the entrance to valleys, near bridges, close to towns, and by ports, but also in some unlikely places. Those in unusual situations would owe their presence to one of two causes. First, they might have been built by some late-comer to royal esteem who had to content himself with land which no one else wanted, and felt obliged to build a castle to demonstrate his importance to himself and to others; secondly, they might have been sited by an ingenious strategist – and Europe bred plenty of them – who visualized flanking attacks on any invading force. The mathematics of this sort of strategy is very simple. If X sets off with a force of ten thousand and invades the neighbouring country Y, he may be confident of victory because he knows that Y has a smaller population and cannot muster any army of more than six thousand. He crosses the frontier without great difficulty for it has no natural obstacles to assist the defender, but runs into considerable problems when he has to go through a pass and a marshy valley. Most low-lying ground was marshy in medieval times. In neither pass nor valley does he encounter more than harassing resistance, but he knows very well that up in the valley sides are two strong castles, and on the edge of the marsh are two more, one of which is almost impossible to reach. The path in between begins to look less inviting, for the moment his main army goes through, its retreat, though not perhaps prevented, will be made very slow and hazardous. His line of communication will undoubtedly be cut. He would have preferred to fight his way in and slaughter a large portion of the enemy, but this he is not allowed to do. As the main danger must come from the garrisons sheltered in the castles, he must estimate the time and numbers required to reduce them. Knowing that they are probably well-sited and that defenders have the considerable advantage of cover, he realizes he must employ a four-to-one superiority in men. He has to estimate whether the garrisons are large or small; whether the main force is waiting for him in the plains, marshes or valleys beyond, or whether there is merely a tantalizing will-o'-the-wisp to draw him on until he is surrounded in inhospitable country. He decides that the risk of leaving these four castles intact in the rear is too great, so he must immobilize them even if he cannot actually take them. He dare not spare enough men for a four-to-one superiority, so he decides – and hopes – that two-to-one will invalidate their threat, and even give him a chance, with luck, to capture them. Assuming there are five hundred men in each castle, he detaches four units of one thousand each from his own force. This has created supply and general logistical problems. He is now down to six thousand men in his main force, he is trying to live off the country, and if he runs into any more tactical problems he will find himself facing a foe with superior numbers fighting over familiar ground with the desperation of men dedicated to preserving their families and homeland. It is a difficult equation and the medieval castle made full use of it. In later years it was to appear on a much larger scale (see figure 1).

Although the medieval strategist would not have known the term, his concept was what is nowadays called defence in depth. Clear understanding of the methods and aims of medieval warfare is necessary if we are to appreciate the events. It is frequently stated that some castles were not captured because they were impregnable. No fortification yet produced has been impregnable, for what may not be achieved by force of arms may be accomplished by treachery, starvation, or even the offer of generous terms. Castles which were not captured were usually spared for excellent reasons. Possibly their potential nuisance value did not merit a long and expensive siege, possibly there were diplomatic reasons why they were spared, possibly there was nothing important at stake and the castle was being besieged in a combat that was as morale-raising as a modern military exercise.

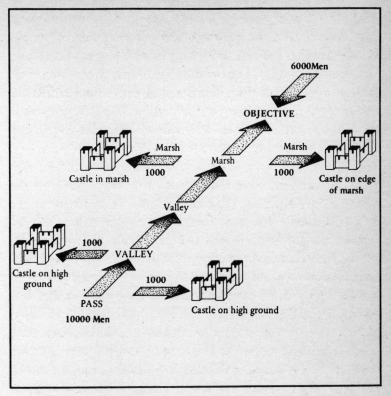

1   How castles draw off numbers from the invasion force

So far we have seen the castle in defence, but it had an equally important function in attack. An advancing army will at some stage have to stop and consolidate; frequently it will need to dig in and prepare for a counter-attack. Centuries of experience have tended to make commanders cautious of long thrusts into enemy territory, but the origin of it may well have been in the days of poor communications when thrustful leaders were liable to find themselves isolated in hostile areas. The castle was a refinement of the policy of digging-in. It provided an observation post, storehouse, recovery centre and residence. Each castle would be within easy reach of others so that one could cover another and, if necessary, provide reinforcements or diversionary attacks. The fact that it was a personal possession in a territory which would soon be parcelled out to the baron and his knights in the form of manors, gave these people a special and urgent reason for holding and subduing the area.

There were then many varying reasons for the number and importance of castles. They could provide a network of defence, or a springboard for attack. They were armouries and ordnance depots, observation points and forward positions, headquarters and homes. They were the most closely integrated form of military and civilian life the world has ever seen. A fortified town was a trading centre adapted to look after itself, a fort was a device with a purely military function, but a castle was a successful combination of both. Dwellers in castles would therefore feel the pride and satisfaction of belonging to a well-organized and efficient establishment.

2

The Precursors
of the Castle

Although the motte and bailey castle appeared on the eleventh-century scene with what appeared to be dramatic suddenness, the castle was not an invention but the result of a long evolution of defensive technique. It was preceded by more elaborate fortifications and ambitious concepts. The story goes back to pre-Roman times when Europe had tribal defences of varying quality.

Outside Europe there had, of course, been complicated and effective fortresses, such as those at Troy, Babylon, Asshur (capital of Assyria), Thebes, Mycenae, Rhodes, Tarragona (Spain), the Great Wall of China, Zimbabwe (Southern Africa) and Yucatan (Mexico). These varied considerably in design and strength but were essentially different in character from the hill fortresses of early Europe, which are usually, though wrongly, called castles.

Pre-Roman fortifications frequently consist of massive earthworks, and the visitor is usually astonished at the huge ditches and embankments which were created on hill tops by humans labouring with primitive tools. Easily accessible are the English fortresses at White Horse Hill, Berkshire; Old

Sarum, Wiltshire; Maiden Castle, Dorset, and Hereford Beacon Camp (Herefordshire). White Horse Hill dates back to the Iron Age; Old Sarum is a concentric fortress of which the outer ring is of a remote, unknown date. Inside the inner ring at Old Sarum the Normans built a castle, now in ruins. The enclosed area is about twenty-seven acres, the central ring being about three hundred feet in diameter. These ramparts are one hundred feet from the bottom of the ditch, which varies somewhat in width, but is mostly one hundred and fifty feet across. Hereford Beacon Camp was built between 400 and 300 BC. Most impressive is Maiden Castle, Dorset. It is believed to date back to 2000 BC, although most of the complicated concentric ditches are 1500–1800 years later.

Formidable though many of these buildings still look, they were doubtless even more so when in use. Some of the early fortresses included walls of timber and stone. When timber and stone are used to make a wall the combination is stronger than when either is used singly. Sometimes as a result of enemy attacks in which fire was used stones became welded together – or vitrified – and formed a wall of immense strength. When timber was used in combination with earth it was usually fireproof provided the filling was solidly rammed.

Although hill forts were ingeniously constructed and were designed to take a heavy toll on the attacker, their builders preferred to confront their enemies in front of, rather than within, the precincts. According to the Romans, who had personal experience, the native inhabitants brought their opponents to battle with a combination of mobile infantry and unpredictable cavalry. The Romans spoke feelingly of the dash, courage and firepower of these opponents, whose ranks contained large numbers of expert slingers.

The establishment of Roman power in Europe changed the military situation swiftly and completely. Spain, France, Britain and Germany were provided with roads, garrisons, and stability. The Romans did not place great faith in fixed defences in outlying stations, preferring to trust to speed and mobility. Their highly-trained forces moved swiftly from place to place, digging what local defences they thought appropriate. Not that the Romans did not appreciate the value of fixed fortifications when necessary. Rome was surrounded by twelve miles of wall twelve feet thick. For most of its length it was sixty feet high, and at hundred-foot intervals had powerful, projecting siege towers. The wall was crenellated and pierced with numerous arrow-loops. Engines for throwing stones and other missiles were placed at convenient points behind.

Less massive but scarcely less powerful defences were built elsewhere. Outside Rome one of the most notable fortifications was at Aosta. This was a rectangle some seven hundred yards square. The walls were twenty-one feet high and massive towers protected the corners. However, in view of its situation – on the north-west – it was not surprising to find it so strong.

Nîmes, in Languedoc, had been used as a garrison town. It has an interesting gateway – the Porte Augusta built in 15 BC. On each side is a semi-circular flanking tower, which could have served as a model for castles twelve hundred years later; the gateway itself had a double entrance, each protected by a portcullis. Double entrances were to be found in other Roman gateways, for it was felt that the extra mobility they provided more than compensated for the inevitable weakening of the defence. Autun, Fréjus and Senlis provide other examples in France; Trier (Germany) has a similar though more formidable gateway built at a later date.

During the third and fourth centuries the Romans built a chain of forts along the south-eastern English coast, with the intention of repulsing Saxon invaders. Impressive remains still exist. At Pevensey (Sussex) and Portchester (Hampshire) the Normans built strong castles in a corner of these Roman walls. Pevensey encloses an area of ten acres with walls twelve feet thick and twenty-five feet high; not least of the impressive features of this formidable structure are the heavy bastion towers. Portchester is on a slightly smaller scale.

The walls of London enclosed an area of approximately three hundred and thirty acres. None of the Roman gateways remain but the foundations indicate that they, as well as the walls, were similar to those in other Roman towns. Colchester, which was an important garrison north-east of London, had formidable defences. The walls were eight feet thick and were backed by a rampart twenty feet wide. Colchester had, of course, taken a bitter lesson, and was probably over-fortified on the assumption that this was one place where history must not be allowed to repeat itself. In AD 61, when the Roman governor of Britain was busy with a campaign on the Menai Straits, between North Wales and Anglesey, the Iceni, who lived in what is now called East Anglia, rose in desperate rebellion. The Romans had no one to thank but themselves, because they had unjustly annexed the lands of the Iceni queen, Boadicea, and even beaten her with rods. The Iceni were joined by others, the Ninth legion was hacked to pieces, and London, St Albans and Colchester were all sacked. For the main garrison town in East Anglia to be burnt and plundered was more than Roman pride cared to think about, and its subsequent defences were designed to ensure there should be no repetition of such a disgrace.

Although the Romans preferred to seek out their enemies

and destroy them in open battle, this was not always possible, particularly when the Empire began to decline. In consequence they undertook the stupendous task of enclosing not merely a town or a country with a wall but a whole Empire. These *limes* or boundaries were stout enough to hold up invaders long enough for the Romans to bring up their reserves to the spot. The *Limes Germanicus* began as an earth embankment crowned with a palisade and watch towers, which followed the line of the countryside. It made full use of additional natural obstacles such as mountains and rivers, and ran from the Rhine to the Danube.

But when Hadrian became Emperor in the second century AD, the old *Limes Germanicus* was not good enough. Apart from any other consideration, there was too much fraternizing with the local people who were all lumped together by the Romans under the one name of 'barbarians'. Hadrian drew a fresh line and built it with stone. In its final form it was as straight as was humanly possible, ran from Coblenz to Eining, and was so strong and menacing as to acquire the nickname 'the Wall of the Devil'. Approximately eighteen hundred years later German and Allied troops fought over the same ground, noting with some surprise that useful tactical positions already possessed ancient but still serviceable stone defences (see figure 2).

Elsewhere there were other formidable barriers. Africa had to be content with a series of walls and forts sufficient to keep out desert raiders, but the Syrian wall built by Trajan between 98 and 117 consisted of a closely-linked chain of castles along the river Euphrates. Moesia (now Bulgaria) was protected by a wall linking the Danube to the Black Sea. Best known of all, perhaps, is Hadrian's Wall between England and Scotland – or, as it was then, between the Romans and the Picts, the untameable painted men of the north who still daubed their

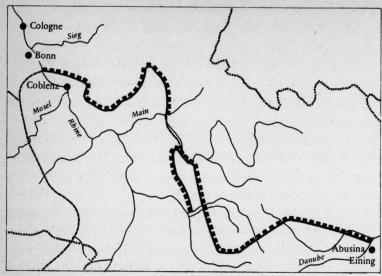

2   Limes Germanicus

3   Hadrian's Wall

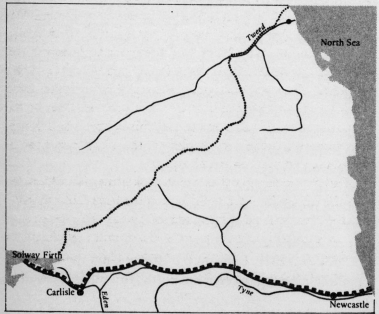

bodies with strange patterns in bright blue woad.

This wall stretched from Solway Firth in the west to Tynemouth in the east, a distance of some seventy-three miles. It was seldom less than seven feet thick and its average height was fifteen feet. Formidable fortresses were built every four miles along its length. On hilly ground it took advantage of slopes to make it more forbidding, but where no slopes were available it was strengthened by deep ditches in front. In the early stages garrisons in walls such as this were neither Romans nor local people, but were drawn from other conquered provinces such as Morocco and Spain. Looking out across the bleak hills, in driving rain and chilly mist, they yearned for the warm sun of their native lands, and often recorded their homesickness and discomfort on the stones of the wall. Later, when Scotland was partially conquered, another wall was built between the Forth and the Clyde. This Antonine wall (for Antoninus was the Roman Emperor at the time, AD 138) was on a smaller scale than Hadrian's but its forts were less widely spaced. It was no less formidable.

However, the stoutest defences are soon overrun if too many troops are withdrawn and the garrison becomes too thin. This, in the decline of the Roman Empire, was what happened. The great walls of the Roman Empire contributed much to the development of military building, but at the same time showed the weakness of this concept of defence. Subsequently, castles accomplished the same task just as effectively and much more cheaply.

Of all the barbarian tribes which took possession of Europe after the fall of the Roman Empire in the fifth century, none equalled the Saxons for sustained toughness. They appear to have originated in Scandinavia, and it is said that their first wanderings occurred when they were hired as mercenaries. By the eighth century they held most of the territory between the Elbe and the Oder, as well as substantial tracts of land in England; the latter are easily recognizable by their names, Sussex, Essex, and Wessex, denoting South, East or West Saxons. They were unshakeably loyal to their own kind, lived by war, would never admit or accept defeat, and when not fighting or plundering were gambling, if not too drunk to do so. Christianity made slow headway among them. They themselves had a mixture of pagan religions and worshipped the ash-tree Yggdrasil. Their faith absolved them from keeping treaties made under duress. The struggle between Saxon and Frank ebbed and flowed, apparently never wearying the patience of the former and never exhausting the resources of the latter. In 782 Charlemagne massacred 4,500 Saxon prisoners in cold blood as a punishment for burning churches and killing missionaries; this had no effect on Saxon resolution either way, but is always regarded as an unfortunate stain on Charlemagne's record.

The Saxons were in Britain before the Romans left. South-eastern Roman castles such as Pevensey and Caister had been built to keep them out, and the Romans had appointed an officer whose title was 'Count of the Saxon Shore'. However, the Saxons continued to arrive and some managed to settle. Once they were on the soil of Britain they got on with the Romans rather better than did the original Celtic occupants. In consequence the Romans favoured them, approved their language and some of their customs, and looked upon them as suitable heirs to their empire in Britain.

After 410, when the Romans had withdrawn their last legions, Britain provided the perfect example of what happens to a country which has insufficient fortifications and a lack of trained manpower to make the best use of available defences. The Romans had used their excellent road system to bring adequate forces to bear on any opposition; the

Britons had neither the training nor the logistical support to make proper use of the Roman legacy and in consequence it was the invader who benefited from the roads, which enabled him to probe deeply into the country. The Picts and Scots from the north were soon raiding deep into the Midlands; the Angles, Jutes, and Saxons had equal success in the south. The invaders burnt and destroyed everything they encountered. A contemporary British chronicler wrote 'famine dire and most famous sticks to the wandering and staggering people – priests and people, swords on every side gleaming and flames crackling, were together mown to the ground . . . and burial of any kind there was none except the ruins of houses, the bellies of birds and beasts, in the open'. (*De excidio et conquestu Britanniae*)

The Saxons referred to their opponents as 'Waelisch', which meant foreigners. The Waelisch were driven to Cornwall, to Brittany (in France) and into what is now called Wales.

But the invaders did not have it all their own way. In 516 at an unidentified spot, but which may well have been the hill on which the city of Bath now stands, the battle of Mount Badon saw the Britons inflict crushing defeat on their opponents. It seems that the Britons used the hill as a fortress and slaughtered the Saxons as they tried to capture it. But for the most part the only successes the Britons had against their opponents were in guerilla warfare. Neither side seems to have had a proper strategy nor been concerned with holding ground. The Saxons eventually won because there were more of them; they loved warfare and destruction, they spread a wave of terror, and concentrated a frenzy of close-quarter fighting on any opposition brave enough to stand up to them. They used the classic tactics which can only be blunted by fortifications at key points along the attacker's route. Later, when they had settled, they took a step toward the evolution of such defences as would have defeated their own invasion, but much blood was spilt before a satisfactory defensive concept was produced.

After the Angles and the Saxons had settled in Britain, and existence had become relatively peaceful, a new and devastating force appeared on the western European scene. This was the Vikings. Their first appearance in England was in 787, for a swift raid on Dorset. Soon the European continent knew them well and dreaded them accordingly. Opinion is divided as to whether they derived their name from 'Wicing' meaning 'warrior' or from 'Wic', the creeks by which they penetrated far inland.

Although all of Scandinavian origin, the Vikings were not a single people, nor did they all follow similar paths. The Danes and Norwegians were essentially seafarers; they were also heathens and professional pirates. No respect for religion inhibited their plundering, and no other occupation interfered with their life's work, piratical raiding. Europe was a simple and obvious prey. They descended without warning in their magnificent and graceful boats; they could sail far inland up shallow creeks, and could depart even more quickly than they came. Retaliation was impossible, for raids were led by relatively unimportant chiefs who were of no value as hostages for good behaviour. And the fact that few towns were defended, and there were no castles, left England and France an easy prey. Soon single craft were replaced by ships in their hundreds, and the Viking bands ravaged far inland. On occasion these forces might be brought to battle but the results were by no means always satisfactory for the intercepting force. Curiously enough, it was the descendants of these people, the Normans (Northmen), who evolved the castle.

Only recently has a clear and fair picture of the Vikings begun to emerge. As accounts of this formidable people were written mainly by those who suffered from their barbaric raids, it is not surprising that posterity rated them as nothing more than resourceful savages. They were known to be heathen, and probably atheistic; they were said to be without culture or any form of ethic. Archaeology has caused a sharp revision of this opinion; for example, such finds as the burial ship at Sutton Hoo in Suffolk show that they were connoisseurs of art as early as the seventh century. But their most notable contribution to the medieval way of life was 'berserkgangr' or joy in battle. This characteristic was retained by the Normans and, allied with administrative skill, enabled them to found lasting kingdoms.

The origin of the distinctive qualities of the Normans is somewhat of a mystery. Normandy itself, as a Romano-Gallic state, had become Christian in the fourth century. During the ninth century it suffered as much if not more than many of its neighbours from the Viking reign of terror. But in the year 911 a treaty was made between Rollo of Normandy and Charles the Simple, King of the Franks. Rollo accepted the portion of land around Rouen, was baptized, betrothed to Charles' daughter, and agreed to do homage and feudal service for his lands.

Rollo appears to be one of those people who leave a lasting mark on history but are themselves almost unknown. Legend has it that he may have been Rolf the Ganger, an exiled Norwegian who had, perhaps to escape someone's vengeance, moved first to Scotland, then Ireland, and finally France. It has been said that he was too heavy (or too tall) for a small Norwegian horse to carry, and this gave him his name of 'the walker'; it seems more likely that he was a 'goer, a wanderer'. The word 'gang' became widely known when Robert Burns,

in the eighteenth century, wrote
> 'The best laid schemes of mice and men
> Gang aft agley.'

and keeps its original meaning in 'gangplank'.

Whatever Rollo's origins may have been, there is no doubt about his aftermath. The Treaty of Saint Clair-sur-Epte, referred to above, gave him a firm hold in Normandy; soon he was in successful conflict with neighbours in Anjou, Flanders, and the Capetian duchy which later became known as the Kingdom of France. The fact that early medieval France was only a portion of the country that bears the name today, and a not very effective portion at that, is confusing to the reader when he first comes to grips with events of the time.

On his death in 933 Rollo was succeeded by his son William Longsword. William managed to extend the ducal territories before being murdered by the Count of Flanders in 942; his successor was a ten-year-old boy named Richard. The boy held his inheritance not because of his own efforts but because his neighbours were determined that no one else should have it if they themselves could not. When he died in 996 Normandy appeared to be settling down as a country of some stability. His successor – another Richard – encouraged religious houses, and earned the title Richard the Good. He was followed by Richard III who lasted one year; the shortness of his reign was said to have been due to a dose of poison administered by his brother, who succeeded him. This brother, known as Robert the Devil or Robert the Magnificent, according to where one's sympathies lay, was the father of William the Bastard, better known as William the Conqueror or William I, King of England 1066–87.

Although there is no doubt about William's illegitimacy (for his father never married his mother), it is worth noting that the Vikings were accustomed to raise families from mistresses rather than wives; bastardy could not therefore be a stigma.[1] Among other people it was a different story, and the sneers that William heard in early youth made him defiant in later years. On a number of occasions he began royal proclamations with the statement: 'I, William the Bastard, . . .' His mother was Arlette daughter of a tanner at Falaise. The story is that she was washing clothes in a stream when Robert's eye fell on her. After producing a suitable successor for Robert she was married off to the Vicomte de Conteville, for whom she produced a dynasty almost as distinguished as the Norman kings of England.

In the years between 911 and 1066 Normandy developed into a country which was capable not only of a stable existence but also of launching an expedition into a powerful foreign country, and methodically subduing it. More than that, it clamped a system of law and order onto its subject people and laid the foundation for centuries of sound organization, stable government and religious progress. The Normans established an impressive though different type of kingdom in Sicily, and later formed the core of the Crusades. As early as 1026 the Duke of Naples allowed a wandering band of Normans to settle in and fortify Aversa, and hold it as an outpost against his enemies in Capua. Others fought as mercenaries in the service of various Italian princes. Troins (Sicily) was besieged by the Saracens in 1063; after four months they were driven off in a desperate sally by the starving Normans. Sicily is, of course, rich in Norman remains. These are astonishing achievements from humble origins, and although this is not the place to examine the personal qualities that made these successes possible it is

[1] Icelandic law provides to this day that there should be no disadvantage from illegitimacy.

certainly the place to examine the methods. The principal factors of their success seem to be the development of feudalism and the motte and bailey castle.

3

The Motte and Bailey Castle

Feudalism did not originate with the Normans. The custom of holding land in return for military service dates back to the declining years of the Roman Empire, but the Carolingian kings of France were the chief architects of feudalism as a means of social and political organization. The essence of it was that society was a pyramid with the king (or duke) at the top. All owed allegiance to the king through the person immediately above, but all, it is important to note, had some rights. In the case of the lowest peasant or churl, this right might only be to justice in his relations with his equally downtrodden neighbour, and precious little from anyone above him.

Once men had land they realized the need to survey it. This meant mobility, and the only means of mobility at this time was the possession of a horse. From the ownership of horses to the development of a cavalry arm in warfare was but a short step.

But the next stage was of even more far-reaching importance. This was the development and use of the motte and bailey castle. Although castles had been used in the east

29

centuries before, they had never had much influence in Europe. The Anglo-Saxons, in common with certain other tribes, had developed a type of fortification known as a burh, but these were not castles in the true sense of the word. They were positions, strategically placed on hilltops, at river crossings or overlooking harbours, which a tribe could use as a refuge in time of emergency. They consisted of strong timber palisades and ditches, but were not linked with any other defensive system. As many burhs were subsequently built over and became towns it is usually impossible to know their exact dimension or character, but at Witham (in Essex) there may be seen the remains of a burh which enclosed an area of twenty-six acres and had mounds and ditches. The endings 'bury' or 'burgh' signify where burhs once were, but their absence does not necessarily mean there was no burh in that place. Towns like Tamworth in Staffordshire, Warwick in Warwickshire, and Bridgnorth in Shropshire were once famous 'burhs'. The essential difference between this type of defence and the castle was that burhs were community efforts; the castle was private enterprise, privately owned *but* under royal licence. It appears, from a decree issued by Charles the Bald, King of the Franks, in 864 that private castles, forts, and enclosures existed at that time, for he ordered that they should be demolished forthwith; however, there can be no comparison between the rudimentary defences of ill-doers in the ninth century, and the tough defensive character of the motte and bailey castles of the tenth.

The first of the surviving motte and bailey castles seems to have been built in the year 990, or soon after, at Mont Glonne, on the river Loire in France. Its measurements are not known, and it is neither possible nor important to establish whether this was in fact the earliest example of what the castle became later. Recent archaeological excavations indicate that all

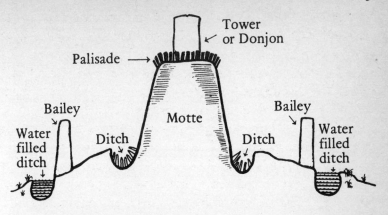

4   Section of motte and bailey castle

motte and bailey castles were by no means designed alike. Some had large wooden gatehouses (for which the postholes have been found); others had the wooden tower built into the motte.

The castles which began to appear all over Normandy in the first part of the eleventh century, and which were an instrument for the subjection of England after 1066, were constructed as follows. The essential characteristic was a large mound, anything from fifty to one hundred and twenty feet high, and from fifty to three hundred feet across at the top. The sides were steep, and the process of excavating earth for the mound created a useful ditch around the base. Where feasible this ditch was filled with water, but some castle-holders preferred a deep dry ditch full of spikes and other obstacles. On top of the mound was a tower, one or two storeys high, and around the edge would be a wooden -palisade. Surrounding the ditch was another wall, enclosing the 'bailey'. During peace the ditch was crossed by a bridge, but in time of siege this was removed entirely. The mound was called a 'motte' from the Norman-French word for turf.

Later the word changed into moat and was used to describe
the wet ditch. Another curious shift of meaning occurred in
the word 'donjon', which first described the tower. It was a
derivation from low Latin and meant dominating point. At
a later stage, when castles were built of stone, and the owner
preferred more comfortable quarters than an austere tower,
the donjon was used for prisoners. Prisoners were still put
in the donjon or dungeon long after towers had ceased to be
built, by which time they would probably have been below
ground level.

The thought of prisoners languishing for many years in
deep dungeons, emerging only for interrogation under
torture, has caught the imagination of modern sightseers. In

5   Castle Acre, Norfolk. The main bailey extends to the left. This is
one of the few castles with a double bailey

consequence almost every room below ground level is labelled as a dungeon. In fact many of them were storerooms for food or weapons. But even less romantic is the explanation of many secret passages underground: they were drains.

To return to the daylight. The motte and bailey castle, however sombre-looking to those it dominated, was painted in vivid colours. A record of this practice is to be found in the name the 'White Tower' for the keep of the Tower of London. In dazzling white this would be visible for miles and would leave no doubt of its presence. Other castles were painted red, green or blue, or all three, both within and without.

Although simple in design, and easy to build, the motte and

6   Castle Rising, Norfolk. The earthworks, which cover 13 acres, are probably pre-Norman. The keep is an excellent example of early Norman work. It measures 75 × 64 ft and is 50 ft high

bailey castle was by no means easy to capture. The steep slopes of the mound were designed to be more than a horse could manage; the dashing cavalryman was therefore denied the opportunity of leaping the barrier and scattering the defence like chaff. Instead he had to dismount and crawl up the difficult slope unaided.

But when defence nullifies one weapon it usually gives vast encouragement to another. It was so with the bow. Although far short of its later potential, the arrow was already a most effective incendiary weapon. Flaming material would be launched onto the palisade, and when defenders appeared in order to douse the flames a further flight of arrows with iron tips would cause heavy casualties. The balance of attack and defence would tilt first to one side then the other. Defenders would cover their palisades with wet hides; attackers would crawl up the mound under similar protection. The attack would use arrows to start fires; the defence, using their superior height to give their bows a longer range, would pick off the assailants before they came close enough to be dangerous.

Our information about the motte and bailey castle comes from many sources but two of them are especially interesting. The first is the Bayeux Tapestry, which relates the story of the rivalry between Harold and William the Conqueror; the second is the account of Lambert d'Ardres, who left a detailed description of an elaborate castle which was built in 1117.

The Bayeux Tapestry is a mine of information. One scene shows the castle of Rennes and another that of Dinan. One of the most interesting scenes shows the motte at Hastings in the course of construction; the mound itself looks like a multi-storey sandwich. This peculiarity of construction was thought to be artistic licence until excavations elsewhere

RETVR:CASTELLVM:AT·HESTENG·CEASTRA

7 Scene from the Bayeux tapestry: building a castle with forced labour. Note dispute being settled behind overseer's back. The tower on the right may be a prefabricated one which was brought over by boat in sections

showed that mottes were often made of a variety of materials and these bound themselves together like a modern road foundation; most of the materials were found in the adjoining subsoil.[1] The wooden tower was shipped from Normandy in sections in special boats. Another curious feature of the same section (see figure 7) is that two of the workmen are having a fight with spades (behind the overseer's back of course). No doubt there were occasions when the labour force, which would be made up of conquered tribes, nurtured stronger hate for fellow-victims than it did for the comparatively new enemy which had forced them into

[1] Silbury, the largest artificial mound in Europe, was found to contain the same construction when excavated in 1968.

slavery. In other sections there are vigorous attacks; cavalry are prominent but the main damage is being done by arrows, or by the bearers of incendiary weapons which look like long torches.

This is the description by Lambert d'Ardres who wrote about a wooden castle which had been built at Ardres in 1117, about seventy-five years before:

Arnold, lord of Ardres, built on the motte of Ardres a wooden house, excelling all the houses of Flanders of that period both in material and in carpenter's work. The first storey was on the surface of the ground, where were cellars and granaries, and great boxes, tuns, casks, and other domestic utensils. In the storey above were the dwelling and common living rooms of the residents, in which were the larders, the rooms of the bakers and butlers, and the great chamber in which the lord and his wife slept. Adjoining this was a private room, the dormitory of the waiting maids and children. In the inner part of the great chamber was a certain private room, where at early dawn or in the evening or during sickness or at time of blood-letting, or for warming the maids and weaned children, they used to have a fire.

In the upper storey of the house were garret rooms, in which on the one side the sons (when they wished it) on the other side the daughters (because they were obliged) of the lord of the house used to sleep. In this storey also the watchmen and the servants appointed to keep the house took their sleep at some time or other. High up on the east side of the house, in a convenient place, was the chapel, which was made like unto the tabernacle of Solomon in its ceiling and painting. There were stairs and passages from storey to storey, from the house into the kitchen, from room to room, and again from the house into the loggia, where they used to sit in conversation for recreation, and again from the loggia into the oratory.

However, it may well have been that this building earned a detailed description because it was almost unique. The majority of motte and bailey towers were very simple edifices. The bottom floor was the storeroom, the middle would house the soldiers, and if there was a third storey it was occupied by the lord and his family. The kitchen was in the open air, not because Normans liked cooking under a rough shelter but because that was the only way to keep the smoke and smells from pervading everything. Yet it would be a mistake to think that this open-air cooking was necesarily inefficient. An experienced camper can produce an excellent meal in the open air, and an ingenious army cook can produce miracles. There is no reason to suppose that their medieval counterparts were any different. A few snowflakes may not add much flavour to a stew, but they certainly prevent it from losing its nourishment by over-cooking.

Men who took a passionate delight in the hardships and dangers of war were unlikely to have set much store by physical comfort, and their womenfolk were as tough as they were, if not tougher. Mabel of Belesme, although not an estimable character, bathed in a river in November and dried off by lying naked on her so-called bed. When medieval castles were abandoned, it was not only because they had outlined their tactical and strategic usefulness but also because men were not like the men that used to be; instead of preferring a secure eyrie on a windswept crag, or a cunningly sited lair in the middle of a dank marsh, they preferred towns, a gravel soil, and what modern estate-agents call 'residential amenities'.

Castle siting at the motte and bailey stage was affected by two main factors: strategy and tactics. Strategy, which is the overall planning of a campaign, required that castles should hold new ground, and, if needs be, support each other. Within this plan, siting would be affected by such tactical requirements as guarding fords, controlling roads, valleys, and land or water junctions, overawing towns, and acting as depots for the storage of men or materials. Sometimes, because of a change in topography, the military historian and the archaeologist have to combine to reach an explanation of why a certain castle is where it is. The military historian will know that the passage of troops was very slow in certain areas; the archaeologist will explain that at that time the river was wider, the marsh wetter, or the forest thicker. Subsequent draining may have changed the situation completely.

From the earliest motte and bailey constructions to the elaborate Edwardian castles one feature was always present; attacking a castle was a hazardous business. The medieval tactician had inherited the lore of ancient predecessors and designed fortresses which would enable the defender to inflict heavy casualties. Medieval warfare was a bloody affair at best, and casualties had to be very high indeed for anyone to take much note of them. The defenders of mottes liked to catch the attackers between the inner and outer defences; later, the chosen killing-ground was usually between barbican and gatehouse. The attacker who pressed on too fast might find himself cut off in an exposed position where he could advance no further and also had his retreat blocked.

As is well known, William, Duke of Normandy, crossed the Channel in 1066 and became William I of England. His victory at Hastings was a narrow one, but it was decisive enough when he cemented it by building a chain of motte and bailey castles across the newly-conquered territory. However, the early years of his twenty-one-year reign were full of alarums and excursions even after the country had a network of castle defences holding all the key positions.

It is also well known – except to those who proudly and often mistakenly claim to be descended from William's companions at Hastings – that the Norman army was mainly a collection of grasping, unattractive mercenaries whose only redeeming feature was their courage. However, William was well aware of how to handle his supporters and bestowed on them huge estates which would both reward and occupy their abilities. Later, there would be occasions when these powerful barons would give trouble to their feudal superior, but in the early days they were fully occupied in consolidating their gains and building their castles. It is instructive to follow the fortunes of a few of them.

As might be expected, there was soon a chain of strategically-placed castles in Sussex, the area where the Norman landings had taken place. Hastings has already been noted; it stood on a high cliff and dominated a wide area. It was given to Humphrey de Tilleul but passed from him to Robert of Eu. Pevensey, which controlled the marshy area, was given to Earl Moreton, and Chichester – to the west of the Sussex Downs – was awarded to Roger of Montgomery. The Montgomery family was destined to play a significant part in medieval and later military history; they were the ancestors of Field-Marshal Lord Montgomery of Alamein.

The three gaps in the South Downs were guarded by Arundel, Bramber and Lewes. Arundel, looking over the river Arun, went to the D'Albini family. The original motte is enclosed in the later castle which is now the seat of the premier duke of England, the Duke of Norfolk. Bramber has already been mentioned; one of its interesting features was the tactical device of leaving a ridge for the attacker to climb on to; then, placed on a narrow platform with ditches behind and before him, he would be fully exposed to missiles from the defence. Such 'killing-grounds' were designed to reduce the number of attackers so that the assault was either called off or could be scattered by a quick sally from the castle. Bramber was held by William de Braose. His descendants, though rich and powerful, would live turbulent lives. The castle was extremely strong, and in 1644, during the English Civil War, sustained and resisted heavy attacks.

Lewes not only controlled a gap in the Downs but also benefited from the river Ouse which at that time was navigable. Lewes was therefore a port as well as a fortress. Although much of the masonry has disappeared enough remains to show what it once was like. There is a very well-preserved barbican. An unusual feature of Lewes is its two mottes. One has no masonry on it and may have been a 'malvoisin' rather than a part of the defensive scheme.

There were of course other smaller castles such as Eastbourne, which has now disappeared completely.

Further north one finds the same story. Along the line of the North Downs are Reigate, Abinger Hammer and Guildford. It was this methodical closing of gaps, denying the passage of fords, blocking valleys at both ends, and keeping watch over all movement, which consolidated the Norman Conquest. Anyone who stands on a motte – any motte – will be surprised at the area of country he can survey. Even if the motte is only a grassy mound, such as at Oxford or Cambridge, the extent of land which can be observed will be surprising. In any area there are often several places which might have been selected for siting a motte yet the Normans, without maps, instruments, or much topographical knowledge, seem to have had an extraordinary facility for picking the best position. All mottes were taller than they are today, for by now the soil has settled and much has been washed away by rain during the last nine hundred years. With a three- or four-storey wooden tower on top, their look-out value probably meant that – except in very hilly country – each would be in sight of at least one other. And even in hilly country this mutual visibility was frequently achieved – as in west Wales.

Lincoln was already a fortress of note when William I entered it in 1068 but that did not prevent him superimposing

the Norman pattern on the Romano-Danish defences. Like
Lewes, Lincoln has two mottes; like Oxford, and probably
in common with many other castles, houses were demolished
to make space for it.

At Oxford it is said that the mound was piled on top of the
existing Saxon cottages, but so far archaeologists have not
yet been able to prove whether this is true or not. Oxford
was a town of some importance and a burh; it was also the
highest point at which the Thames was navigable. The castle,
on the west of the town – but now unfortunately in the prison
precincts though easily observable from the road – was built
by Robert d'Oilly. It was completed in 1071, doubtless with
a wooden tower. Later, a stone keep was built on this motte
but, in the way of heavy buildings on artificial mounds, gave
endless trouble. A seventeenth-century print showed the
tower as having an enormous crack; it disappeared, with all
its masonry, soon after.

By the side of the mound is a square Norman tower,
stepped and battered. Officially it is the tower of St George's
church, but militarily it is a superb tower ideally situated to
guard the lower side of the castle. The castle was surrounded
by a moat. Subsequently this was filled in and buildings
erected. Some of these lean at curious angles although they
have not been up many years, and it is said that builders and
architects all chose to ignore the proffered advice of archaeologists and historians. In 1142 Queen Matilda was besieged
in Oxford castle by King Stephen and, according to the story
which varies a little in the details, was lowered by a rope one
wintry night – or slipped out through a postern – with three
accompanying knights. As it was snowing they were dressed
in white and, after evading the piquet, walked six miles on
the frozen Thames to Abingdon. There they obtained horses
and rode another ten miles to Wallingford.

As some castles had two mottes so did others have two – or
even more – baileys. The bailey or ward extended the area
of the fortifications and therefore made the way of the
attacker longer and more arduous. It was also the area which,
when a siege was pending, would be crowded with stores,
peasants and refugees.

The shape and position of the bailey depended on military
conditions and the lie of the land. At Windsor there was a
bailey (ward) on each side of the keep. This was necessary
because the excellent natural motte had too much flat ground
above and below it for safety. Although now a royal palace,
Windsor gives an excellent impression of how a medieval
castle functioned. It has a massive gateway, steep cliff-like
slopes to the north, a chapel, residences, inhabited flanking
towers, and soldiers on guard. The mound, long thought to
be artificial, is crowned with a shell-keep – which was raised
by thirty feet in the nineteenth century for the sake of
appearance. A shell-keep was created by building a stone
wall round the upper part of the mound, much on the lines
of the old palisade. Shell-keeps distributed the weight and
could be used where to build a stone tower would be to court
disaster. Other notable shell-keeps may be seen at Trematon
and Restormel in Cornwall. At Berkeley in Gloucestershire,
the castle in which Edward II was murdered in 1327, the
entire motte was enclosed in a stone shell. This total enclosure
of the motte was probably not as original as was subsequently
thought, for archaeologists have now uncovered traces of
timber revetting on mounds that were long thought to
consist of earth only; the revetting may have been necessary
because the soil needed support in the early stages, but may
have been a sensible application of the timber and earth
combination used so effectively in pre-Norman days.

The word 'keep' was rarely used in medieval times,

'donjon' being preferred. Keep implies watching over, as in 'gamekeeper', and doubtless came to be applied to the donjon for that reason. It also means a residence; to this day Cambridge undergraduates use the term 'to keep' to denote living in lodgings.

Considerable confusion has surrounded the study of early castles. This has been due to lack of proper co-operation between archaeologists, military experts and historians. This is sad but not surprising. Excavating a small motte such as Hen Domen in Montgomeryshire can take ten years, and there are hundreds like it but not perhaps identical. Military experts are subject to their own particular prejudices, and usually prefer better-documented campaigns. Historians – in this field at any rate – have tended to be more concerned with demolishing each other's theories than in studying the subject inductively.

It now appears that the Normans, excellent though they were at warfare, made mistakes like anyone else. Many of their castles were brilliantly sited; others were not. They had no objection to using an earlier fortification, such as Old Sarum or Pevensey if it suited them; at Brinklow, in Warwickshire, the motte may well be an old burial mound. They used castles to consolidate victory and to extend it. Thus, being adaptable people, they built small mottes where they were necessary and larger edifices where they wanted to impress politically as well as militarily. In mountainous country they used peaks, in wooded country they made good use of timber, and in the west – where timber was scarce – they used stone because it was available. Sometimes they built the tower in the middle of the top of the motte, at other times they made it into a gatehouse at the summit. At South Mimms in Hertfordshire, where Geoffrey of Mandeville built a castle in the twelfth century, the wooden tower was enclosed inside the motte, which was then revetted with timber (it is believed). It is, of course, understandable that in times of anarchy – to which Mandeville largely contributed – a man might wish to build an absolutely secure retreat. South Mimms must have been a formidable defence, for inside the ditches, which were deep, would be sheer walls. On top would be a palisade and behind that the top of the tower, protruding from the mound, useful both for observation and as a platform for crossbowmen.

Very few stone castles were built in the eleventh century but those that were are still impressive. There is the Tower of London, Colchester, and Richmond in Yorkshire. Pevensey also had a stone donjon. Building in stone was a lengthy and expensive business, and the subsequent inevitable repairs would be extremely costly. Stone buildings had a rubble core faced with ashlar (square stone blocks). Occasionally stone was imported from Caen, and examples may be seen at the Tower of London and in Canterbury Cathedral. Caen stone was soft and easy to work but once in position hardened like iron. However, the cost and labour involved with Caen stone was excessive.

Military history is full of examples of lessons that have been learnt painfully in the past, but are forgotten and then learnt even more painfully over and over again. It is not therefore surprising that techniques of fortification are frequently despised or disregarded, and then agonizingly evolved once more.

The Normans conquered England, Ireland, Sicily and parts of Italy with motte and bailey castles. Sited in the best areas from both strategic and tactical points of view, they were excellent military headquarters. But as the Normans settled down they needed larger, more commodious, and more permanent structures. The castle became more than a mere fortress; it had to serve as a home, a court, an administrative and judicial headquarters, a storehouse and perhaps a refuge.

The castles which replaced mottes assumed that the attack would come from one quarter only, and would progress from outer to inner bailey and thence to the donjon. The outer bailey would be crowded with stores and animals, and its fall would bring starvation a stage nearer. The inner bailey would offer stout resistance but before long that too would fall. The donjon offered interesting possibilities because by this time the attacking force would probably be much diminished. If the siege had been long some of the attackers would have been killed, others would have deserted, and yet others would have been called away for urgent agricultural work. The final stage therefore would produce a vigorous conflict between a desperate garrison with only a hangman's rope to look forward to, and a frustrated attack that might at any point become outnumbered. Alternatively, it might produce nothing at all, for the besiegers might weigh up the cost of the final assault and find they were unable to meet the bill in either human or material terms.

High-cost sieges which were fought to a finish were usually the outcome of a king's need to prove his authority. The castle-holder was invariably a powerful baron whose defiance of royal power must be checked before other princelings decided to follow his example. Originally he might have been arrogant and insulting but later would have become uncooperative and probably provocative. The eventual result would be a state of anarchy, as happened in England in the reign of Stephen.

Three remarkable high-cost sieges took place in England. Kenilworth held out for a year during 1265–6 and only surrendered because disease had broken out among the garrison. The strength of its position lay in the fact that it was

surrounded by 111 acres of water. Every expedient was used
in the attempt to subdue it; devastating barrages would be
succeeded by the offer of unexpectedly mild terms, and when
the latter were rejected night attacks and water-borne
assaults would follow.

Forty years earlier King Henry III had been engaged in a
different but equally important siege. This had taken place
at Bedford, where the stump of the motte may still be seen,
but where little else survives to show how difficult the assault
must have been. (There is, however, an extremely fine model
of the original castle and its surroundings in the nearby
museum.) Bedford Castle was held by one Fawkes de
Bréauté, a mercenary who had performed useful service to
the monarch in the previous reign. Unfortunately for all,
Fawkes de Bréauté had become both arrogant and defiant, a
process which culminated in his capturing and imprisoning a
royal judge. Bedford had to be reduced and no pains or
expense were spared in the process. Crossbows, quarrels,
caltraps, weapons, missiles, engines and men were brought
to Bedford from all over England. Wine, which seems to
have played an important part in most sieges, was brought
to the site in vast quantities, and so were sporting dogs and
other recreational aids. Not least of the extravagance which
characterized this siege was that shown with men's lives.

Rochester, which was besieged by King John in 1215, was
not as expensive as Bedford or Kenilworth, but made up for
it in the intensity of the fighting. The three months which the
siege lasted saw little respite. Had the siege been conducted
at a more leisurely pace the royal forces would have won
with much less effort; instead, both sides hurled themselves
into hand-to-hand conflict at every opportunity. This type
of bitter siege usually ended in the defeated being hanged, as
happened here.

4

The Weapons of
Attack and Defence

In eleventh-century Europe the square keep appeared to be the final sophistication in military architecture. But, as often happens, the 'ultimate weapon' can be outmoded with breathtaking speed. It was so in the twelfth century. In 1096 a Crusade had set off from Europe with the laudable purpose of liberating the holy places of Christendom from the control of the heathen. The Crusading ideal had a widespread appeal. It appealed to the knight who enjoyed fighting and was very happy to have a legitimate cause in which he might gain awards or distinction, and to the Church as a cause which kept barons out of mischief. It received the blessing of the Popes who saw in it a means of creating a universal church, and to many soldiers it was a convenient practical way of obtaining absolution for a lifetime of sins. Not least of its attractions was the fact that it offered novel outlets in the way of amorous adventure and debauchery.

Like most of the glamorous events of history, the Crusades had their dark side. In the earlier Crusades all sorts of pious optimists set out with little preparation and no idea of what was involved. The losses from disease, hunger or misfortune

47

were enormous. Peter the Hermit raised a Crusade from the simple peasants of France, but all died before reaching Jerusalem. Even more depressing is the account of the German Children's Crusade; most of the young Crusaders were sold into slavery en route. The First Crusade, which was the most successful, ended in an appalling massacre of the inhabitants of Jerusalem.

But the Crusades, although failing in their main objective, caused considerable changes in European castle architecture and castle life. Middle Eastern towns and castles were the heirs to a long tradition of military architecture, and were vastly more sophisticated than anything that Europe had produced. The first person to make full use of this knowledge was Richard I of England, who built a castle which was the wonder of his age. This was the Château Gaillard in Normandy, and it was thought to be impregnable. Richard was killed elsewhere before the castle was finished, but when it came under siege it lasted six months only. However, as we shall see later, the fact that Château Gaillard disappointed many of its supporters does not mean that it was not a magnificent achievement for its time.

The Crusades stimulated interest in the technical detail of fortification, but it is untrue to portray the castle-builders of late twelfth-century Europe as mere copyists of Muslim builders. They ignored or rejected some features of the Eastern castles, and they adopted, and sometimes improved, others. And they were not beyond thinking out new ideas of their own. The hoard or brattice was a European invention. It was a wooden platform built out from the battlements, from which stones and other missiles could be dropped through slots in the flooring. The growing habit of siting castles on flat ground demanded other new ideas from the builder. He responded with extra thick walls – up to twenty

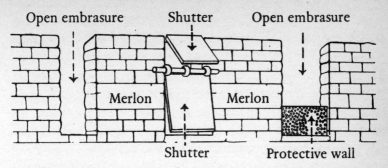

8   Battlements

feet in the lower storeys – and with crenellated battlements instead of plain parapets. The embrasures or openings in the new battlements were two to three feet wide and often had a sill wall as much as three feet high. The remainder of the battlement, known as the merlon, would be from five to six feet wide and six to ten feet high. In the early days the merlons were solid stone, but after the twelfth century were pierced with arrow-loops. Experience soon taught castle architects to shape the top of the parapet to prevent arrows glancing and ricocheting from the parapet onto the defenders. Even then the battlements were hazardous. They became less so after the introduction of shutters, which were hung on hinges from the top and gave sufficient cover for an archer to take his time over selecting a target below.

Although stone was destined to replace wood it was not invariably more efficient. Early stone buildings proved to be more vulnerable to the battering ram than wood had been. This liability was eventually overcome by the establishment of deep battered plinths. A plinth is a supporting circle of stonework round the base of a wall or column, and the term 'battered' denotes a wall that is thicker at the base than the summit. The provision of an outward slope at the base of the wall gave another advantage to the defenders; missiles dropped from above would ricochet into the faces of the attackers who were advancing under cover with a battering ram.

Attacks on stone castles were made in four ways: missiles, arrows, and slung stones devastated the battlements; climbers would try to scale the walls; starvation would weaken the defenders physically and morally; and sappers would undermine the structure.

The disadvantage of taking a castle by mining was that the process could not be anything but slow. To impatient commanders – who might have every good reason for their impatience in that time was against them – assault by miner was the least preferable of all attacking methods. Furthermore, there would be certain sites – where castles were built on solid rock or were surrounded by marsh and water – where a miner would be completely useless. The first step therefore would be to breach the defences. The battlements would be pounded with stones from a variety of engines, and an assault party would creep up to the base of the wall with a battering ram. The part of the building most vulnerable to the battering ram was obviously the doorway, but this would also be the most heavily guarded and probably the most difficult to approach. But assuming that the ditch had been effectively filled in and all traps removed, the combination of a shower of arrows and slung stones along the battlements, the occasional direct hit by heavy stones on the same piece of masonry, and the steady thump of the battering ram at the gateway or base of the wall, would soon begin to show results. Slingers were particularly important: their ammunition was plentiful and could be used in whatever quantity the situation demanded; even if they did not actually drive the defenders off the battlements they could at least reduce their effectiveness; and they could goad the defence into the dangerously rash acts which men sometimes perform when they are harassed and hurt. Escalade, or the scaling of the walls, also took a variety of forms. Sometimes the attackers used a kind of drawbridge, or even beams, based on an assault tower; at others they would hook ropes onto the battlements, or climb ladders constructed on the lattice principle. There have always been intrepid people who can climb walls with or without ladders, and the Middle Ages had an apparently inexhaustible supply of them. Their most impressive characteristic was not, however, their courage or ability but their speed. Hands which suddenly appeared on the battlements would be chopped off, heads would be split

9   A type of scaling ladder

with a sword. But there would always be more hands appearing, and unless the defence was surprisingly nimble hands would be quickly followed by heads and then bodies. Soon it might be the defender who was desperately trying to retain a portion of the battlement and as likely as not being hurled over the side.

Nevertheless, despite his slowness, the most dangerous of all the attackers was the sapper, or miner. His activities had been feared from the earliest times. In the Everyman edition of *Herodotus,* translated by G. Rawlinson and edited by E.H. Blakeney, the following passage occurs (the year is 510 BC):

So the Persians besieged Barca for nine months in the course of which they dug several mines from their own lines to the walls, and likewise made a number of vigorous assaults. But their mines were discovered by a man who was a worker in brass, who went with a brazen shield all round the fortress, and laid it on the ground inside the city. In other places the shield when laid down was quite dumb; but where the ground was undermined, there the brass of the shield rung. Here therefore the Barcaeans countermined and slew the Persian diggers.[1]

Barca eventually fell, not from assault but from trickery and treachery. The Persians exacted a fearful vengeance on the Barcaeans for murdering a man called Arcesitaus. Sieges in the Middle East usually ended in scenes that convinced even the most timid that death in battle was preferable to defeat or capitulation.

Europe, as far as is known, did not make much use of vibrating brass but did, on a number of occasions, utilize another Middle-Eastern device. This was to place pans of water on the ground and watch the surface, which would indicate the slightest vibration made by miners underneath. This method of detection had the drawback of only being

[1] The method seems remarkably like ASDIC – the Anti-Submarine Detector used by the Allies in World War II.

possible when the tunnellers were already under the citadel. Late detection did not matter if the miners intended invasion, but was disastrous if the mine was only for the purpose of bringing down the walls. The technique of this, used over and over again, was very simple. A considerable cavern would be hollowed out beneath a wall or corner tower. The roof of the excavation would be propped in case mild subsidence should alarm the dwellers above, and then the cavern would be packed with inflammable rushes, soaked in animal fat or even petroleum. At the given moment the mine would be set alight; with luck, the intense heat would crack the walls and bring down the buildings above.

The underground miner was not an easy opponent to tackle. The ideal way to drive him out was by countermine and flooding, but this was not always possible. Smoke was often used – it is remarkable how many modern horrors, from gas to napalm, were anticipated in pre-Christian times: 'Greek fire' was fully as deadly as napalm. If the miner could not be driven out by 'scientific' means there was no alternative but to use manpower. But fighting underground, in the dark and in a confined space, is an unpredictable activity, and gains might be less than losses.

The miner was almost as formidable above ground as below it. On the surface he crept up under a covering, and used a pick to bite a way into the corners. He was careful to weaken rather than breach; otherwise the wall might come down on top of him. Subsequently a fire of brushwood or a well-aimed blow from a battering ram would complete the task. Very often a corner would bring down a section of wall with it. It soon became obvious that as long as corners existed miners would play havoc with them. The remedy was soon found – eliminate the corners. In consequence, rectangular towers were replaced by circular towers, and soon the spaces in between were filled with yet more towers giving scope for flanking fire.

When, in the early stages, castles were made of wood and placed on tall artificial mounds, they were seldom occupied for long periods. Their owners moved around and, on the whole, lived a nomadic existence, like Henry II of England, of whom it was said that he even ate on horseback. On his eternal journeyings he would stop anywhere, appropriate one, sometimes the only, habitable building and leave his court to fend for themselves. And this was in the twelfth century. By Henry II's reign most European castles were stone constructions with a strong keep, thick curtain walls, strong corner towers and wide ditches. There were losses as well as gains in this type of construction. They took longer to construct, were expensive to maintain, and because of their heavy masonry could not be built on soft ground. Although artificial mounds did carry masonry when the years had allowed the soil to settle, nobody felt too confident about the balance of structure and foundation. In general, castle-architects went for what builders call 'virgin' – soil that has not suffered from man's depredations. The Tower of London, a massive stone structure, was built on flat but firm ground. Other areas, such as Lewes, could provide strategic sites which also dominated their surroundings. But, in general, the pattern of castle-building after the twelfth century was to rely less on the site than on the architect.

In the heyday of the motte castles – and they continued to be used when the military situation demanded up till the fourteenth century – fire had been the chief danger. Around the top of the mound was a timber palisade entwined with thorns, a formidable obstacle in any era and against any foot-soldier, but vulnerable to the incendiary arrow or the intrepid warrior who would crawl up the mound with a blazing torch. The best that the defender could do was to soak the wood with water, if he had it, or cover the outwork with damp hides.

The epoch of stone did not displace fire as an attacking weapon, but it altered the methods of use. The first stone buildings were square, had no entrance at ground level, and often had the first dozen feet of elevation packed with solid earth. Later, this basement might be hollowed out to make storerooms or prisons. The building was called a turris or tower, and the Tower of London preserves the meaning to this day. Fighting was conducted from the battlements, and if there were apertures further down they would be for light and ventilation, not archery. Occasionally a window would be inserted, but this would be protected by a heavy iron grille, useless to the defenders except for light and air.

Arrow-loops gradually developed from these ventilation apertures. Before the longbow revolutionized warfare the main weapons were bow and crossbow. The bow had a short range but could be useful. It was fired vertically. The crossbow had a much greater range but was slower; it was fired horizontally. In consequence we find arrow-loops were cruciform (in the shape of a cross) and thus designed to suit both weapons. The openings at the end were called oilets; they were most ingeniously cut in the stone and greatly increased the manoeuvrability of the bow. Much later they were replaced by broader apertures, known as gunloops, but guns

Plain   Croslet   With oilets   From above
                    (openings at ends)

10   Different types of arrow-loops

produced considerable problems with their noise, fumes, and
vibrations that eventually did more harm to the stonework
than the opposition could manage.

Battlements were also modified in the light of experience.
The inner side was merely protected by a low sill; this meant
that if a hostile force broke through it would be completely
exposed to fire from other points of the interior of the castle.
This rampart walk was known as the 'allure' and was not
wide enough to hold more than a few men at a time. The
principle of allowing your enemy to reach an untenable
position and then demolishing him was widely observed,
although it was not necessarily practised on the battlements.
At Arques (near Dieppe) and other castles in Normandy,
including Gaillard, it was the custom to leave a flat mound
on the far side of the ditch.[1] This would be contended for,
but eventually occupied by the enemy. From then on, this
exposed platform would make a perfect 'killing-ground' for
those opponents who liked to try their luck in occupying it.

Above the parapet would be a conical roof. Most of these
have now disappeared, giving .the tops of castles a flat
appearance that the medieval soldier would have found
unfamiliar.

At the base of the walls there would have been a battered
plinth. Eventually, however, thickness was not considered
to be a sufficient defence and galleries were introduced from
which arrows could be fired at ground level. These were
necessitated by the heavy protective coverings of siege
engines which were virtually invulnerable from above but
which could be discouraged by the discharge of incendiary
arrows at point-blank range. This area was no place for a man
of claustrophobic tendencies. At any moment a mine might
go up beneath him, a battering ram come crashing in from the

[1] Compare Bramber.

front, or several tons of masonry, the result of a lucky shot by a siege engine, crash down on his head. But some survived, and there were plenty of volunteers to replace those who did not.

Out of sight but never out of mind were the miners. Gaillard was mined because its rock foundation was soft enough to be hacked away, but there were plenty of foundations that defied the sharpest pick and most determined sapper. Moats were essential if there was any chance of the miner getting to work, but, if there was no danger of mining, a steep, dry ditch full of diabolical spikes and other contrivances was preferable. Miners would tunnel from a considerable distance, carefully concealing the entrance, and removing the soil to a safe distance under cover of darkness. Counterminers would, of course, be equally active, and on occasions when one side broke into the other's galleries the fighting underground would be fiercer than that above. (The classic example was at Melun in 1420 when even tournaments were fought in the excavation, but there were other occasions when the miners' galleries were used for personal combat.)

For walls which could not be mined or otherwise broken there was nothing else but the scaling ladder or the siege tower. Although scaling ladders varied considerably the general principle remained the same – to get a grip on the merlons and keep it there. The whole art of using a scaling ladder was speed, a good climber was up a ladder before the defender could dislodge its hooks from the battlements, and there were usually half-a-dozen crossbowmen or slingers to give covering fire. Even so, mishaps did occur and there was not much hope for the man who slipped. At the siege of Caen in 1346 an English Knight, Sir Edmund Springhouse, slipped off the ladder and fell into the ditch. The French threw

11 A siege tower (after Viollet-le-Duc). The moat has been filled up with logs

burning straw over him and roasted him alive as he lay there.

Owing to the association of the word with churches, the impression has grown up that belfries derive their name from the bells they house. The original meaning of 'berfrei' was a shelter, and a siege tower was precisely this. In medieval times they tended to be two or three storeys high, but there are impressive accounts from Roman times of belfries that were twenty storeys high. They were usually assembled a short distance from the site on which they would be used, and were pushed forward on rollers or wheels.

Needless to say, the defence would prepare an adequate reception, which included concealed pits whose covering would give way as the tower moved forward. Once stuck in one of these traps the tower was useless and would probably have to be dismantled. When such mishaps did not occur the belfry would proceed forward over a filled-in ditch and previously levelled ground until it was near enough to lower a drawbridge on to the battlements. The scene in the confined space must have been confused and dangerous, but intensely exciting. By this time there was a fair chance that the defenders would have set some part of the belfry alight in spite of its being protected by wet hides; and retreat – although probably never contemplated – was made impossible. From the lowest storey a battering-ram would be crashing to and fro. As belfries grew taller, castle walls and towers grew up to match them, until the fourteenth century saw such dominating construction as Caesar's tower, 147 feet, and Guy's tower, 128 feet, at Warwick Castle, which would dominate the tallest belfry and be beyond the reach of the strongest missile. (Neither tower has anything to do with its namesake; both were built by the Beauchamps when they held the Earldom of Warwick in the later 1300s. As we have noted, Caesar's has that little extra inner tower that recalls the keep at Château Gaillard.)

Battering-rams and bores took two forms and had a variety of mountings. Some had a spiked head which bit into the stonework; others had a flat end which cracked the surface. All but the smallest were suspended in slings, and as

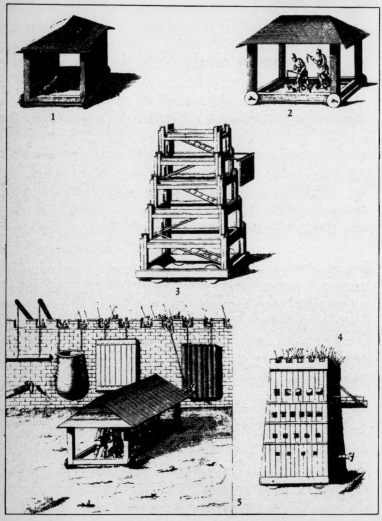

12   Machines used in ancient sieges: 1 and 2, covers for surface miners; 3 and 4, assault towers; 5, ram under cover. Note the protection mats against the walls and the defenders' attempts to seize the ram's head with a grapple

some were large tree-trunks fitted with a steel head handling them was an enterprise involving as many as a hundred men. Generally, but not invariably, the blunt-headed implements were known as rams, and sometimes were tipped with a crude representation of a ram's head. There was considerable

13   Battering-rams with different heads, two with spikes; from Grose's *Antiquities*

art in timing the movement of the carriage and the swing and twist of the ram in the slings.

Meanwhile, the activities of the ram party did not go unhindered by the defence. Stones, fire, boiling water and red-hot iron bars rained on to them, pads of sacking were lowered between the ram and the wall, and hooks and pincers would be dropped on to the ram's head, neatly imprisoning it. Protected by iron plates and hides, the ram looked like some huge animal butting and gnawing away at the base; in consequence it was nicknamed the 'sow', the 'cat' or the 'musculus' (mouse).

The efficiency of the sow meant that special attention had to be paid to the gateway, which was originally the weakest point in the structure but in the fourteenth century became one of the strongest. Gates were protected by flanking towers and drawbridges. When the latter was raised it not only removed a bridge but also gave double protection to the doorway behind. Although many drawbridges were raised on chains some swung on a pivot, thereby creating an obstacle in front and a pit behind.

However, as a few blows from a tree trunk might well dispose of drawbridge defence, there developed an outer structure known as the barbican – a word of obscure origin. This consisted of further towers sometimes connected with the gatehouse, sometimes separated and some way forward from it.

By the time the barbican had been developed, considerable thought had been given to the problem of defence in this quarter. The entrance road was transformed into an ambush area so that once past the outer works the attacker would have great difficulty in extricating himself if he decided to retreat. The assault party would be channelled and funnelled along the only possible route for entry but that route would be so full of hazards that the invader would have little chance of reaching the far end – if most of the building was still intact.

At all stages and points in the attack there would be a constant volley of small-arms fire. By no means the least effective part of this would come from slings. Although not glamorous weapons, these had long been known for their deadly effectiveness. Ammunition was plentiful and could be used without stint. Volleys from slings could be delivered in such rapid succession as to provide a continuous rain of missiles; a man appearing on the battlements might well be greeted by a hail of stones such as might nowadays be pro-

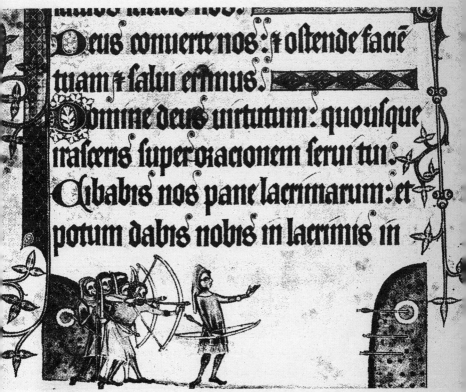

14 Archery practice with longbows from the Luttrell Psalter

duced by a hundred or so powerful catapults performing simultaneously. The only drawback to this deadly weapon was the skill and practice required for its efficient use, but there is ample evidence that on numerous occasions it was a highly efficient, almost decisive, weapon.

The bowmen were not at first very highly rated. In the

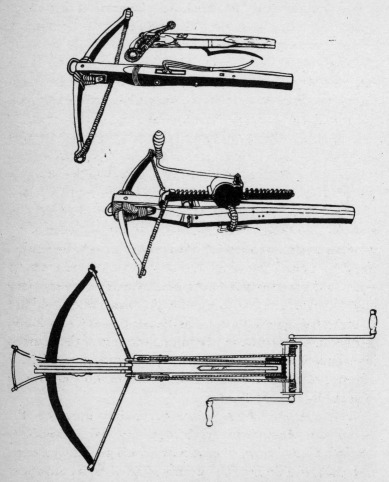

15   Crossbows: *top* lever crossbow; *centre* ratchet crossbow; *below* rolling purchase crossbow. The winding apparatus is detachable

early days of the Norman invasions the bow was merely drawn back to the chest and had a short range. Even so, it assisted the Norman victory at Hastings when King Harold of the English received an arrow in his face. By the late eleventh century a more deadly weapon was widely available – the crossbow, a weapon which had been used by the Greeks and Romans but which had been out of favour for many years. This was banned by the Church at the Lateran Council of 1139 as being too inhuman to be used by Christians against Christians. The judgement of what is fair and what is not fair in war makes an interesting study. In the eleventh century it was fair to chop a man to pieces with an axe but not fair to shoot him from a distance. In the twentieth century it is unfair to poison his drinking water but quite legitimate to blow him to pieces. However, banned or not, the crossbow made great headway. In the twelfth century it was made of wood but later, by the fifteenth century, made of steel. The crossbow was the application of machinery to archery. The string was pulled back by using a lever or by winding a crank on a ratchet. By this means far more tension could be gained than could be obtained by muscle power alone, and a crossbow could be used by a sick man or even a boy. Unfortunately, it was a slow performer and could not be protected against the rain – as the Genoese at Crécy found to their bitter sorrow. Furthermore, the cost of the quarrels (crossbow bolts) was high and their waste prodigious. By the fifteenth century they were mostly of steel and had a range of about five hundred yards.

There is an interesting selection of crossbow quarrels in the Fitzwilliam Museum in Cambridge, and also a stonebow. The latter was a form of crossbow which propelled a stone and was probably nearly as deadly as an ordinary crossbow without being so expensive in ammunition. There are also pavises, which were wooden shields which archers used for protection when they were rewinding their bows. They were about five feet high and three feet across, and were often slung across a man's back when not in use. It was not uncommon for an archer to tie a string to his bolt before firing at an opponent's pavis. As soon as it struck he would jerk the string and pull the pavis over. One of his companions would then discharge a bolt into the exposed target.

Although well known in Wales earlier, the longbow did not become popular in the rest of Britain until the thirteenth century. It was a deadly instrument, but took much skill and practice to use. A trained man would fire twelve arrows a minute over a range of 240 yards. A body of six thousand archers – as at Crécy – would therefore open the assault with 72,000 arrows in the first minute, and most of them would find targets in men or horses. Strict accuracy was unimportant when dense flights of arrows were fired at close-packed formations, but at shorter distances in slower timing the results were surprisingly deadly. But the longbowman had to practise till he was sick of it – practise to keep his muscles in trim, practise to improve his aim, practise to make him steady under all conditions. Not even the Roman legionary had so much military exercise. When shooting from cover his first shot had to tell, for this arm movement would give him away, just like the bolt action on an old-fashioned rifle. Another disadvantage was drifting with the wind; a gusty day would demand considerable skill in aiming off. Even so, the longbow was a better weapon than a musket until the Battle of Waterloo, and it was convenience, not efficiency, which caused its premature replacement by firearms.

Behind the small-arms came the artillery. Siege engines took a variety of forms but may be roughly classified as

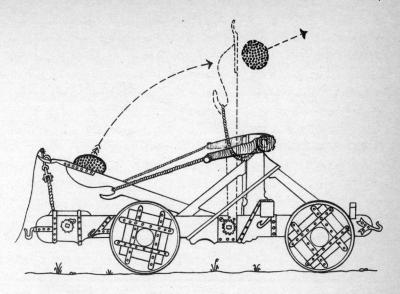

16   Reconstructed siege catapult: a form of giant crossbow

being worked by tension, by torsion, or by counterpoise.
Weapons which worked by tension were in effect giant
crossbows. These became known as 'balistas', although in
fact the word originally referred to torsion weapons.

The second variety of weapons depended on twisting, and,
like the tension weapons, used horsehair or human hair –
which is more tensile. (Horses, incidentally, established
themselves in men's affections in the Middle Ages when they
were found to have a peculiar affinity for battle, to become
excited and spirited at its prospect and to bite and kick
opponents.) Torsion weapons could launch considerable
weights. They acquired the name of 'mangonels', from which
we derive the word 'gun'. Weapons were usually stones
weighing up to five hundredweights, but occasionally were
other offensive missiles, such as a dead horse from whose

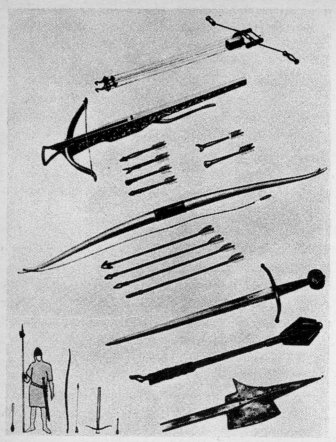

17   *Top to bottom* Weapons of the crossbowman, longbowman, and man-at-war. The windlass-and-pulley system shown above the crossbow was a neat method of cocking the crossbow after each shot, but it took far more time than drawing a longbow. Shown with the crossbow is a variety of bolts. The size of the longbow at centre would vary with that of the archer. His arrows, at first flat-headed and deeply barbed, were eventually given a heavy streamlined head like a rifle bullet, which had a far greater penetrating power. Broadsword and mace were the weapons of both mounted knight and man-at-arms. But in the later Middle Ages the heavy-headed pike (*bottom*) was emerging into a key infantry weapon which would survive long into the seventeenth century. *Left* Some comparative sizes

putrid carcass it was hoped disease would spread.[1] Conventional missiles may be seen in quantity at Pevensey Castle, Sussex. The stone balls which are piled in heaps were recovered from the moat, and are the relics of some long-forgotten siege.

The heaviest artillery was provided by the trebuchet, a huge machine which worked on the counterpoise principle. Sometimes this depended on an enormous weight, but at others the lever was swung by men pulling on ropes. The gun crews of these ingenious weapons were called 'gynours' and were of course a constant target for the archers and slingers of the opposition.

In addition to these main weapons there were a host of other ingenious devices. Even pigeons were used to carry incendiary material.

From 3000 BC fire had been recognized as a decisive weapon in siege warfare. Unfortunately – or perhaps fortunately – the ingredients of Greek fire were less readily available in Europe than they had been in the Middle East, but a considerable quantity seems to have been used. The formula for perfect Greek fire may be as much of a legend as the recipe for alchemy but, short of perfection, there were some very useful recipes. Accounts of 'Greek fire' suggest that petroleum and oil formed a large part of its constituents, for it would burn on water, and developed intense heat. Bitumen, sulphur, resin, naptha and pitch may well have figured in some recipes. One formula could apparently be blown through tubes. But its main use was to make incendiary arrows, which were used as late as the siege of Bristol in the English Civil War in 1643.

Our forbears were not content with the simple mixtures that do duty for napalm or phosphorus grenades – theirs

[1] The French launched dead horses into the castle of Thin in 1339.

were more sophisticated. Sulphur would make incendiary material stick to surfaces, quicklime would make it ignite on contact with water, and pitch would make it burn longer. Quicklime was, of course, an invaluable material. Scattered down wind it could blind an adversary, poured over a scaling ladder it could penetrate chinks in armour, and if placed damp in pots and left in a building could make an interesting time-bomb booby-trap. Red-hot sand was sometimes used as a substitute and was remarkably effective at penetrating the vizors of knights climbing scaling ladders.

But incendiary material and 'Greek fire' were not without their defensive counters. The first requirement was not to panic, the second to obtain supplies of vinegar, sand or even urine (which contains potash) for quenching the flames. Even psychological warfare, which took the form of spreading the belief that the use of Greek fire was unchivalrous and therefore unworthy of a true knight, was not without its influence.

It is extraordinary to think that such a widely-used weapon can have had its secret so well preserved (unlike most modern military secrets). Possibly the explanation may lie in the fact that the formula was extremely simple but required the addition of some essential oil or vegetable fat, which would be familiar to spies but whose particular potency would not be appreciated by them.

5

A Castle at War

The achievements of twelfth-century military architecture were seen at their best, as we said above, in the
Château Gaillard. A full understanding of Château
Gaillard demands some background knowledge of the
contemporary political situation. When Henry II of England
married the enormously rich Eleanor of Aquitaine, divorced
wife of a King of France, it did little to improve relations
between the English and French crowns. The marriage
produced four sons, two of whom died at an early age, a
third, Richard, who built Château Gaillard, and a fourth,
John, who lost it. Richard was a formidable warrior, and has
been elevated into a heroic national symbol. The facts are
somewhat different from the legend. Richard's ten-year
tenure of the English throne was one of continuous absen-
teeism, for he spent approximately eight months of his entire
reign in England. Nevertheless, his reputation tended to keep
most of his subjects loyal; an exception was his brother John.

If Richard has been over-praised by romantic writers, so
John has been over-vilified. With a mother like Eleanor of
Aquitaine and an absentee brother like Richard it is not

surprising that John nursed a few private ambitions. Richard's haughty behaviour had made him well-hated among his contemporaries on the Crusade, and the demands of his administrators made him unpopular in England. It seemed a golden opportunity to John when Richard was imprisoned by his enemies on the way home from the Crusade. In a highly competitive field the chief hater of the English king was probably Philip Augustus of France. Technically, Richard owed allegiance to the King of France for both his Norman and his Aquitaine dukedoms but he showed little sign of acknowledging it. Philip Augustus was therefore inclined to support the intrigues of John, who, he thought, might be more amenable. Part of the bargain was that John should hand over certain Norman border lands, which included such powerful castles as Gisors. Unfortunately for John's schemes, the plan miscarried; Richard was ransomed for an enormous sum and on his return drove John and his plots like chaff before the wind.

But Gisors had gone and Normandy was open to French attack. Richard, a fighter to his fingertips, decided to turn a necessity into a virtue and built a superb castle guarding the approaches to Rouen. It was brilliantly sited and incorporated the best of the old architecture with some excellent new ideas but was not as revolutionary in design as it has often been proclaimed to be; it was perhaps a sign that a revolution in basic design was necessary. But even after Gaillard's weaknesses had been exposed we find certain English and Welsh castles (Pembroke, Beeston (Cheshire), Chepstow and Corfe) being built to a similar pattern in the next few years.

Château Gaillard (Gaillard = saucy) was built on a three-hundred-foot-high spur of ground at Les Andelys, overlooking a curve in the river Seine. Earlier castle builders had laboriously raised a mound of earth, or scarped a hill; later

18   Château Gaillard: the wall of the inner bailey (note the convex
surfaces, to make breaching difficult)

19   The keep of Château Gaillard

siters merely cut off a spur with a deep moat and treated the detached portion as a hillock. The traditional aspect of Gaillard was that it treated defence longitudinally; the attacker had no alternative but to approach along a narrow peninsula over rough ground, cross a moat, bring down a wall, fight through an outer bailey, cross another moat, take yet another bailey, reach one more moat, breach a wall, and if the resistance held out – storm a keep. This was defence by attrition; soon it would be replaced by defence as concentrated destruction at the outset of the attack.

The innovations of Gaillard were not considerable enough to make it impregnable, but they were useful. Brattices, the wooden hoardings that had already proved themselves, were replaced by stone and given the new name of machicolations. Unlike later versions they were supported on buttresses, although it must have been obvious to the architects that those buttresses would prevent effective flanking fire. Below were deep battered plinths (mentioned earlier) which would both strengthen the structure and cause missiles to rebound and ricochet among the attackers. Every surface that could be made oblique, including the keep, was made so, in order to defeat missiles. Many of these refinements had been pioneered at La Roche Guyon (Seine-et-Oise).

Another interesting feature of Château Gaillard is the distance to which the towers project from the wall of the outer bailey, although, in the event, this was no safeguard against the operations of the miner. The drawbridges were of the pulley type and therefore not particularly effective. The keep had walls twelve feet thick, and projected like a ship's prow. The ultimate refinement was in the plinths in the lower part of the walls, for the lower part was oblique and the upper concave; in consequence, missiles would be given fan-like deflection.

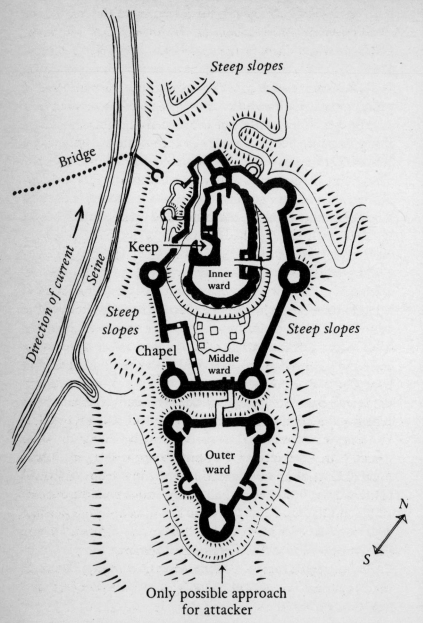

Steep slopes

Bridge

Direction of current →

Seine

Keep →

Inner ward

Steep slopes

Chapel

Middle ward

Steep slopes

Outer ward

N

S

Only possible approach
for attacker

20   Ground plan of Château Gaillard

Richard's defences included the denying of the river Seine to all traffic down to Rouen. Unfortunately, Richard never had a chance to defend the citadel he had built. If he had lived, his castle might never have been attacked; Philip Augustus was brave but not foolhardy. But Richard died of a gangrenous arrow-wound in 1199 and John, who preferred mobile to static warfare, was left to defend Gaillard.

It is, of course, unnecessary to waste pity or exculpation on John. He was a completely ruthless self-seeker whose only virtues were courage and administrative ability. When Richard 1 died the strongest claimant to the throne was Arthur, the son of his eldest brother. But Arthur was a sixteen-year-old boy of no experience while John was a wily and experienced old campaigner. In the circumstances it could only be a matter of time before Arthur disappeared from the scene. As matters turned out, this event was delayed by the revolt of the French barons who preferred the ineffective rule of a weak boy to the powerful grasp of astute John. The naïve young man, unaware that they were interested in their own welfare and not in his, made a willing tool. Philip Augustus was bought off from Arthur's side by being given territory but continued to supply knights to the rebellion just the same. Eventually Arthur was captured in the siege of Mirebeau,[1] where he was besieging his own grandmother, Eleanor of Aquitaine, who, as ever, was John's loyal aide. Arthur disappeared into the dungeons of Rouen castle and was never seen again. Speculation about the manner of his end has gone on ever since but it seems quite possible that he was starved to death; John was addicted to this economical way of disposing of his enemies.

The disappearance of Arthur had far-reaching effects. It was exploited to the full politically in both England and

---

[1] The relieving army is said to have covered eighty miles in two days.

France, but in the latter it also gave force and direction to the
military effort. Every self-seeking and self-righteous baron
was profoundly shocked by the deed and hastily looked
round for whatever political or territorial advantages he
might grab in the general uproar. Philip Augustus realized
this was a heaven-sent opportunity, appointed himself the
champion of the dead boy (whose claims he merged with his
own), summoned John to attend the French court, con-
demned him in his absence, and then declared him to have
forfeited all his French territories.

It was clear to all, and to none more so than Philip
Augustus, that John would not retire merely because he was
told to. The French King therefore set out to eject him.

Curiously enough, John made no effort to tackle Philip in
the field. Instead he dallied at Rouen, drinking and ranting,
while the French king occupied most of the countryside
without resistance. Why John allowed his opponent to gain
this initial advantage is a mystery, although it was readily
explained by contemporaries as being due to a curse of
apathy resulting from the foul murder of his nephew.
Eventually, when apathy gave way to action it merely sent
him scuttling back to England.

But in August 1203 the main prize of the war was still to
be won. Philip had advanced down the Seine towards Rouen,
knowing as he went that the way was barred by the magnificent fortress that Richard had built seven years before.

The outer ward of Château Gaillard, which the attacker
must assault first, was an isosceles triangle with sides 175 feet
long and a base (facing the middle ward) 125 feet long. Each
corner had a forty-foot-high tower, with walls eleven feet
thick. Along the curtain wall were smaller towers for
flanking fire. The tower at the apex of the triangle was
particularly powerful. Outside, separating the castle from

the rest of the ground, was a ditch thirty feet wide and twenty feet deep. According to William le Breton, Philip Augustus's chaplain, who was present at the siege, this forward tower was mined and breached. However, the masonry is intact and the rock beneath has never been disturbed by miners. The breach referred to was obviously made in the adjoining curtain, but the claim shows how necessary it is to check the reports of enthusiastic eye-witnesses against the site of the scenes they purport to describe.

The middle ward was approximately oblong, being about 325 by 200 feet. This, while preserving the longitudinal manner of defence, introduced a form which became standard practice years later – the concentric method. Concentric fortifications have each defence line enclosed by another, but at each stage outwards the walls are lower. The defenders are therefore able to direct a very heavy volume of fire on the approach roads. If possible, the spaces between the respective lines of approach should be too narrow for an attacker to concentrate adequate numbers for the assault on the next wall; he will then be at a disadvantage against the defenders, who already dominate him from the battlements and flanking towers. This principle was used at Gaillard, where the middle ward enclosed the inner ward and the inner ward enclosed the keep. Inside the battlements of the keep there was a further tower, probably of timber.[1]

The inner ward, measuring 100 by 200 feet, was shaped like the human ear and had a novel construction in that seventeen convex buttresses made the work of the miner extremely difficult. The keep was neither round nor square, as was usually the custom, but of an entirely original design. It appears to have been built purely for a desperate, though unlikely, last stand, for it had neither staircase, fireplace,

[1] Caesar's tower at Warwick castle has the same principle, but in stone.

garderobe (latrine) nor well.

In spite of the provision for a final stand and no surrender there was a postern leading out of the inner ward to the outer, and thence to a hilly path. Posterns were designed to give the defenders of a lost cause a chance to escape, but in practice were seldom successfully so used. They were rather more efficient in facilitating sallies and enabling attackers to be caught in the rear. At the top of the towers were the machico-lations, mentioned previously, projecting on corbels; they were the first stone ones to be seen in western Europe. Through slots in the floors of the machicolations the defenders could shower down stones, hot water, red-hot iron bars, hot sand, quicklime, and other anti-personnel material.

Like most castles, Gaillard was built of flint rubble bound together by cement whose tenacity has lasted over seven hundred years. The walls were faced with ashlar, i.e. square stone blocks; and the appearance was one of great strength. It is understandable that Richard is alleged to have said 'Behold my fair daughter, how beautiful she is!'

Needless to say, the approaches received considerable care and attention. Slopes which were already formidable were shaped to make them unclimbable, and towers and walls were built to dominate the valleys. The river passage was denied to all but friendly craft by a fort on the island in the middle, and this in turn was linked by a bridge to further fortifications on both sides. In addition there was a stockade of three rows of piles across the river. The aim of this last manoeuvre was to prevent hostile craft using the river to bypass the castle and slip by downstream.

The castle and its supporting works probably took at least three years to build, and was not finished when Richard died in 1199. John's contribution was to build a chapel; and it was from the crypt of this building that the downfall of the castle was accomplished. Of that, more later.

Having arrived on the site, Philip proceeded to make a long and careful reconnaissance of the military situation. Like Richard, he was a keen student of Vegetius, a writer of the later Roman Empire whose observations became the classic Field Service Pocket-book of medieval strategists. Vegetius believed in hard training and meticulous preparation; he also believed that a good general would come to battle only when he was certain of victory. Philip Augustus began by capturing the opposite bank, which was a relatively easy task in view of John's apathy. This, of course, was the point at which Philip should have been checked, and would have been if Richard had been alive.

The next task was to destroy the bridge and its defenders so that he could replace it by a pontoon manned by his own men. William le Breton gives a graphic account of the battle. 'Weapons rained down on them like a hailstorm, stones, beams, jars of burning pitch and masses of iron.' We are given a comprehensive account of the casualties:

Another, as he dies, collapses in the middle of the boat on his dying comrade, and gives him his last embraces and rejoices as they go down, comrade with comrade, to the infernal regions. Another is deprived of a foot, another of his eyes, another of his ears. One falls with gushing entrails, one with his throat cut, there a thigh is shattered by a staff, here brains are scattered with a club. One man's hand is shorn off with a sword, another forfeits both knees to an axe. And still none draws back from the fight until the pitch poured from above causes them to step back. One groans as he breathes his last from a sword stroke in the face ...

And so on. Grim though it may sound, this is a truer picture of medieval warfare than romantic legend conveys.

There was a huge beam at the edge of the bridgehead, a square mass of immense weight which two teams of ten bulls could hardly shift on a wagon. This, launched on them from above, surprised the two boats and shattered both prows. Then for the first time they retreated. Defeated they take to flight. In the whole army, excluding those who have already met a violent death, there is not one whose body does not bear some wound.

Le Breton goes on to describe the continuation of the fight on the water. The aim is clearly to seek out and destroy. Certain fighters are mentioned by name. One of them is such a skilful swimmer that he can go for miles (!) under water. This man fills some pitchers with live coals, seals the openings and tars them over, then tows them under water till he reaches a point underneath the ramparts that line the shore below Gaillard.

He emerged into the shallows and started a fire from that part of Gaillard's crag which looked towards the citadel, where there were no defenders, since they did not foresee the possibility of danger to themselves from that quarter, and had devoted their main energies to those sectors on which the enemy was exerting the most pressure.

This intrepid swimmer was a pioneer frogman; his modern counterpart attaches limpet mines to warships. The resourceful man of great courage who finds an unprotected way into the most redoubtable citadels seems to crop up in every age and every country.

Le Breton describes the ensuing fire with poetic rhapsody:

Without delay Vulcan grips the wooden ligatures of the wall, and all those walls of the fort which adjoin the town area. It was helped by the sunny weather and the blasts of the east wind . . . it consumed palisades, ramparts, and houses, and all scaffolding which gave protection to the walls.

This event, which greatly raised the morale of the attackers, had precisely the opposite effect on the defenders. The inhabitants of Little Andelys, a township which had grown up under the protection of the castle, abandoned their homes and took refuge in the fortress. Philip promptly occupied the evacuated town and held a celebration festival of martial games, for which there were huge cash prizes. The occasion was stated to cost one thousand pounds a day.

John made one attempt to lift the siege, entrusting the difficult task to the Earl of Pembroke. The relief was to take the form of a land attack on the French forces and a water-borne assault by seventy boats which also carried food for the besieged. Unfortunately for the English the timing went hopelessly wrong, and the French were able to annihilate first one force and then the other. After that, John departed for England and left the castle to fare as best it could.

Philip then decided to establish a strong headquarters on the mainland from which he could not be dislodged by one of the garrison's sallies. At the same time he made sure that Château Gaillard itself was effectively blockaded. The castle was under careful surveillance by day and by night, although this meant troops bivouacking in the open. The watch was so well-organized and so thorough that it became a legend celebrated in popular song. Such disciplined close-picketing was, of course, thoroughly contrary to medieval practice, when arrangements were usually loose and haphazard. There is no doubt that Philip Augustus's conduct must have seemed a little over-zealous, even unsporting.

The commander of the English garrison was Roger de Lacy, whose family had won considerable military renown in the Welsh Marches. As soon as de Lacy saw the blockade tighten he realized that this was a fight to the finish. He was experienced enough to know that the work that the French troops were doing would keep them fit, and the assault, when it came, would be vigorous. Doubtless he too had read Vegetius. It was obvious that the inhabitants of Little Andelys were now a liability and not an asset. Before the 'circumval-lation' they had been able to slip out at night and bring in

food, but this was no longer possible. He promptly pushed
the first five hundred 'useless mouths' through the gate

> . . . to go wherever fortune might take them. And after a few days he
> arranged to drive out as many again, those whom the hostile troops
> pitied and did not wish to condemn to death, as beggars and wretches, a
> mob useless for war. The King [Philip Augustus] heard this and after-
> wards allowed no one, rich or poor, to leave the fort. And as many as
> were sent to them from inside the fortifications were to be driven back
> with darts and javelins in order that they should still consume food.

In medieval sieges, especially of towns, it was sometimes
the custom to allow non-combatants, i.e. the elderly, the
sick, or children, to pass through the besieger's lines. At the
siege of Calais in 1346 Edward III allowed the first batch of
non-combatants through his lines and even gave them food
and money. But when a second contingent appeared later
.they were neither fed nor permitted to pass, and died in slow
agony in the no-man's land between the two armies. The
fate of a non-combatant was not an enviable one; if pushed
out of the besieged fortress he was likely to die of slow
starvation and if he remained inside would almost certainly
be massacred if it fell.

Roger de Lacy then 'mustered separately those men who
were capable of fighting. For these he reckoned the food he
had would amount to a year's supply'. The rest, twelve
hundred of them, were sent out of the camp. 'He had no
doubt he was sending these wretches to their deaths, nor did
he care what fate overtook them provided he could save the
fort for a short time.' The rabble, as Le Breton described
them, streamed out like a flight of bees. Soon their joy
changed to sorrow, for the French drove them back with
spears and javelins. They rushed back to the gates only to
find them shut and barred.

Le Breton spares no detail of their sufferings. Cannibalism

broke out and a bird which fell among them was eaten
feathers, feet and all. Dogs and rats stood no chance whatever.
However, before recoiling too violently in horror from these
events it might be remembered that dogs were not unknown
in the medieval diet, and that starving people do not necessarily eat anything, and in many cases will not relieve their
hunger by foods to which they are not accustomed. There
are examples of rice-eaters starving to death because they
would not eat the wheat which had been provided by famine
relief organizations.

The unfortunate wretches who were pinned between the
attack and the defence hung grimly on to life until Philip
Augustus inspected the forward lines. When they saw him
they begged for bread and mercy, both of which they
received. It was obvious that they could now do neither good
nor harm to anyone. Such scenes as these, when non-
combatants were expelled from castles but not allowed to
reach the besiegers' lines, were a not infrequent occurrence
in medieval sieges.

With the arrival of spring, Philip Augustus decided he
could wait no longer. His men had already been in the field
for six months and that in itself was a costly enterprise. But the
greatest problem was not the cost but whether he could keep
them in the field. The key to medieval prosperity was
agriculture, and unless men tilled the fields in the spring
there was nothing to come at the end of the year. Armies had
a habit of melting away at the beginning of the sowing
season as well as at harvest time. The only troops who could
be relied upon were mercenaries, and even they would
disappear if food, pay, and success did not come along in
adequate quantities.

The early stages of the attack proceeded as might have
been expected, for it was a conventional situation and Richard

had probably not expected the outer ward to do more than take the edge off the assault. Philip spent some time levelling the ground, a fact which William Le Breton expresses somewhat poetically: 'The earth is ordered to abandon its rocky mounds, in order that there may be a way from top to bottom.'

The road, once made, is used for the transport of missiles, tree trunks, turf, and anything else that can be used to fill in the castle ditches. Soon, multiple catapults are also in position and begin to launch a deadly rain in missiles on to the castle walls. The defenders throw back heavy harassing fire from darts and javelins, so much so that the attackers are forced to build protective screens of hurdles and stakes. Next, belfries appear; these are multi-storey towers from which the attackers can inspect and fire down on the defenders. It seems that these were a rough and ready affair, for they are described as 'with branches roughly lopped'. Perched at the top were renowned crossbowmen whose marksmanship in previous campaigns had earned them villas, goods and money. Needless to say, this was not all one-sided. Garrison snipers were taking their toll of the attackers; slings, catapults and other war engines were as active from inside the castle as outside it. The technique of sniping was well organized. Every time a door or window opened inside the castle someone put an arrow or dart through it.

Philip Augustus was frequently up in the front line, 'helmeted, every day exhorting now these, now those, coming up to the edge of the ditches, warding off with his buckler arrows and darts which whistled thick and fast about his ears, and bedded themselves in his shield'. This account of the French king's personal bravery should not be discounted as having been written for the sake of public relations; medieval kings were very much addicted to plunging into the thick of the fight.

However, it was the miner and not the missile which made the first breach. With great difficulty a cavern was hollowed out under the curtain wall, the space was filled with props, brushwood and other combustibles. The intense heat under the hollowed-out foundations caused the wall to crack and fall. 'It produces a great roar as it collapses . . . a cloud of smoke whirls upwards in a twisting vortex with mixed flame and smoke and the ruin belches out a great dust cloud that mushrooms out above.'

The garrison's response was to set the rest of the outer ward alight, burning anything that might be remotely useful to the enemy in a frenzied 'scorched earth' policy. But the French were soon through the breach 'roused by the shouts of men and the braying of trumpets'. The function of trumpets was to signal a charge.

But the middle ward was a tougher nut to crack than the outer, and there seemed no way past its moat and up its walls. Among those ceaselessly prowling round on reconnaissance was one Bogis,[1] who with five other cut-throats believed that where there's a will there's a way. They may have been helped by some local knowledge, but the upshot was that they crawled up the steep slopes on the west side and eventually reached a window in the crypt under the chapel. This was the chapel and crypt which did not appear in Richard's plans but had been added by John in 1202. (The importance of this fact is that without this feature the castle might very well have withstood all the physical force Philip could have brought against it, although it would doubtless have succumbed to starvation eventually.) Le Breton glosses over the fact that the intrepid soldier had to crawl up a drain to get at the window.

[1] A name signifying 'Little nose'.

Once inside, the attackers raised a great clamour hoping to cause dismay among the garrison. The latter, however, responded by trying·to smoke them out. In the general confusion, with smoke blowing everywhere, the storming party emerged, rushed to the drawbridge and let it down. As the French swarmed into the middle ward the remainder of the defenders hastily transferred themselves to the inner ward (wrongly called 'the donjon' by Le Breton).

But Gaillard became progressively tougher as the attacker moved inwards. Once more there appeared to be no way past the deep ditches and steep walls. Even a vast siege engine, nicknamed 'Cabulus', was unable to make much impression on the stout convex walls.

Again it was the sapper who saved the day. Richard had, unwisely as it turned out, left a tongue of rock to act as a bridge across the moat. It might well have been that he planned to annihilate attackers as they tried to storm over this in small numbers, but in the event it was put to a different use. The French sappers, who would otherwise have been hopelessly exposed, were able to crawl under its shelter, and began to bore a hole through the base of the walls. However, before the operation had gone very far it was detected and a countermine started from the other wide to come in from above. Although the attackers were forced to withdraw before they had completed their plans to fire the wall, the structure had now been considerably weakened by their activities. Cabulus continued to belabour the wall with huge missiles and, as may have been expected, the inevitable crack appeared. From that stage it was not long before a substantial portion of the wall fell, but while the defenders manned the breach the French appear to have slipped in through the now neglected mining tunnel.

The final stages produced the usual, but unsuccessful, dash

for the postern. By this time both sides were so exhausted and the fighting space so confined, that only four people out of several hundred were injured. No attempt was made to make a last stand in the keep, probably because by this time all hope of relief had been abandoned. Although there are a few examples elsewhere of defenders being driven to the keep and then rescued, these happenings were not likely to occur while John was in his present apathetic mood. There appear to have been one hundred and forty men in the final surrender. It was said, though not by Le Breton, that the crowding in the inner ward was so great that men could not raise their arms to use their weapons, and that exhaustion and frustration were more notable than heroism as the last bastion finally fell.

Castles like Château Gaillard usually play a recurring rôle in history, and once a sombre note is struck it tends to recur. As soon as the siege was over, Philip Augustus set about rebuilding the fortress and making it stronger than ever. Like many castles, it soon became notorious as a prison, but never more so than in the reign of Philip the Fair in the early years of the fourteenth century. Philip's reign extended from 1285 to 1314 and included the best and the worst that could have been expected from any medieval monarch. He wielded great power throughout western Europe, instituted the first Parliament in France, and conferred numerous liberties and privileges on his subjects. By devious means he contrived to dominate the Pope, and had him transferred from Rome to Avignon. This extraordinary period of French domination of the Papacy long outlasted Philip's lifetime and became known as the 'Babylonian captivity'. It had begun with a dispute over Church revenues, had led to the imprisonment of the then Pope, Boniface VIII, who was insulted and ill-treated by the French Chancellor, reached a more civilized stage with the election of a French Pope, Clement v, and in general underpinned Philip's dubious financial position.

An outcome of these events was that Clement handed over the Order of the Templars to Philip, and it seems that Philip not only plundered their resources but also tortured and murdered many of the knights. From that event the curse that ended the royal line of the Capets was said to stem, but equal claim to bestowing the curse might well belong to the Jews whom Philip plundered and expelled from France, and to the inhabitants of Flanders, whom he systematically drained of their wealth and mercilessly ill-treated.

It should therefore come as no surprise to learn that Philip's sons were no less revolting than he was, and that a considerable drama was staged around them. All three were married but no male heir ensued – this, of course, due to a curse from one of the bodies mentioned above. However, the three sons interpreted their misfortune differently and merely assumed that their wives were barren. A change of partner would doubtless have a more fruitful result, but the Church would permit a divorce only if the wives were guilty of infamous behaviour. One wife only, Jeanne, was acquitted, and this fact was not so much due to her innocence as to the fact that she was heiress to the rich province of Franche-Comté. The others were not so fortunate, both being sent to Château Gaillard where they were imprisoned in the cells in the crypt referred to in the siege. The aim of the punishment was to extract a suitable confession which might sound plausible. Blanche proved amenable and was duly divorced (although doubtless innocent). She was released from Gaillard to spend her remaining years in an abbey. But Marguerite, a girl of great beauty, was all too clearly innocent and trusting, and therefore had to be disposed of in another way. She was visited in her cell, wrapped in her shroud and strangled with her own hair. She was twenty; her ghost is said to haunt the château still.

Gaillard was again under siege in 1419 when it was captured by the English in the Hundred Years War. The French retook it in 1429 but soon restored it to the English, who held it till 1448. In 1580 it again stood a siege, but by the end of the century it had been decided that Gaillard was too much of a temptation to the casual adventurer and its demolition was ordered. Fortunately the plundering of the castle for building materials did not go far (for there was a dispute over which neighbouring abbey should have the lion's share), and it is still possible to visualize what it was like in its days of greatness and trial.

6

Training and Recreation: the Foods they ate

When not fighting, the medieval campaigner was thinking about his next encounter, and probably training for it. As medieval warfare depended less on tactics than on personal skill and bravery, it is not surprising that tournaments were regarded as practice par excellence. These were essentially a medieval European institution and did not appear until the eleventh century. Tournaments were miniature battles between troops of knights using lances; jousts were single combats which began with lances and continued with axes or swords. The former was a war game in which the only concession to safety was to point the lance at the body and not the head; the latter was an exercise in exhibitionism mainly designed to impress the ladies, although sometimes to pay off a grudge too. Tournaments were also known as Round Tables,[1] a name derived from the four hundred feet of circular flooring on which they took place. Sometimes several thousand men would be involved at the same time. Practice for both sports took place with the

[1] Mêlée was another word for tournament, but now has descended to describe an untidy brawl.

quintain, a wooden figure shaped like a man holding a sword, which was suspended on a pivot. The object was to strike the figure between the eyes with the lance, but any misdirection of aim would cause the quintain to spin and clout the rider as he passed by. Variations would include covering the unskilful with sand or dousing him with water. However, jousts were not always taken in play, and there are examples of *Joûtes à outrance* or fights to the death, in which unblunted weapons were used. Even when no harm was intended, fatal accidents could occur. Jousts and friendly tournaments were liable to flare up into something much more serious at a moment's notice, particularly if treachery was suspected, and this led to their unpopularity with monarchs who disliked seeing their closest supporters engaged in mutual extermination. At a tournament held near Cologne in 1240 sixty combatants were said to have been killed. Violence among the gladiators was likely to be reflected in violence among the spectators, much as it is today at football games. In 1250 a tournament at Brackley, Northamptonshire, resulted in much ill-feeling. The following year tournaments were forbidden by royal decree, but they went on none the less.

The scene was brilliantly spectacular. The lists were decorated with flags, banners and bunting. Everybody wore full finery and it must have resembled a combination of Ascot Races and Henley Royal Regatta. Varlets were given the difficult, and at times dangerous, task of steadying their masters and, if unhorsed, extricating them from the mêlée. Varlets were not, as is popularly thought, rogues or menials, but well-bred youths who had passed beyond the schoolboy stage but had not yet become esquires. They were a form of medieval cadet, and would endure injury or insult without complaint to reach the cherished next stage in their careers.

The year 1251, in which Henry III prohibited tournaments in England, saw a memorable encounter at Rochester. A number of foreigners had been invited to take part and the English knights, keenly aware of the treatment they had often received abroad, resolved to pay off old scores. Small heed was paid to the niceties of chivalry and in no time the wretched foreigners were fleeing for refuge in the town. Xenophobia is not an invention of the twentieth century.

Dress for tournaments takes us into the subject of armour. Originally this had been a form of chain-mail worn over boiled leather, which in itself offered surprising resistance to sword cut or spear thrust. Subsequently a better solution was found in plate armour, which would cause blows to glance off. In the early days, jousting armour was light and it was therefore possible for an armoured knight to vault from the ground into the saddle, but later when jousting became a royal sport, and armour had to be made safe, the weight increased so much that the rider was helpless when unhorsed. (See Appendix D.)

Warlike kings like Edward I and Edward III of England favoured tournaments although, from personal experience, they knew only too well how they could develop. Foreign entrants were encouraged, and in spite of the unfortunate incidents at Rochester in 1251 continued to take part in jousts and tournaments in other countries, even in those organized by kings or dukes with whom their own king or duke was officially at war. These occasions often had a true international flavour, as when fifteen English knights took part in a tournament arranged by the King of Bohemia, but held in Condé in northern France.

A curious feature of medieval warfare was the single combat that would take place between two armies or in front of a besieged castle. Froissart records such an entertainment that took place before the walls of Rennes, which the English were besieging in 1357. The fight provided for three lance thrusts, three strokes with a battle-axe, and three thrusts with a dagger. This could well have been more exhausting than it sounds. The elevation of the battle-axe to the status of a tournament weapon is an interesting example of how weapons could rise or decline in knightly favour. At the time of the Norman expansion – in the eleventh century – the battle-axe was held in low esteem. By the time of Richard Coeur-de-Lion, not much more than a hundred years later, it was accepted as a kingly weapon. The dagger also rose from being the weapon of poor and despised troops, but has long since declined from favour.

Froissart's Chronicles are a mine of information for medieval warfare, customs and life. They describe a variety of contests and we note from these that the number of permitted strokes per weapon was increased first to five and later to ten. The last would appear to become a form of endurance rather than skill, for manoeuvring around with a battle-axe would be exhausting in itself without its fore-runner and sequel. Holinshed quotes an interesting grudge-fight between the Scottish Earl of Crawford and the English Lord Wells, which took place at London Bridge on 23 April (St George's Day) 1398. The contestants hit each other squarely on the first course and came to a shattering halt. Wells was knocked half out of his saddle but Crawford remained so rigid that the spectators protested he must be tied in. Crawford heard their protests and disdainfully vaulted from the saddle to the ground and back again. Such a display of agility silenced the spectators, and it was not surprising that in the third course Wells was knocked clean out of his saddle and badly hurt.

As might have been expected, the science of heraldry

expanded greatly and became important as a result of tournaments. The duty of a herald was to announce his master, issue challenges, look after prisoners, and identify the dead on battlefields. Substantial ransoms might depend on their knowledge and skill, and it was a grievous occasion for them when a potentially valuable prisoner had his head clubbed off by some churl. Unfortunately for their labours, arrows often found the wrong targets. But by the fifteenth century heralds were indispensable. Shields, crests, and precedence were highly complicated affairs; coats-of-arms, which had originated from simple devices worn on shields, like the colours of a football team, had now become a mass of quarterings, crests which had signified chiefs by a glove or a flower were now elaborate headpieces, and the laws of precedence had a neo-legal significance. Henry v of England (1413–22) made his heralds check all armorial bearings constantly.

But by the 1400s tournaments were too frequent and too hazardous. They had passed beyond the stage of entertainment and were often the cause of quarrels involving whole families. Steps were taken to render them less dangerous, and, since much of the bitterness seemed to stem from the fact that deep wounds were given in what was intended to be a game, attention was first paid to suitable protective covering. Some of the armour in current use was found to be inadequate, and to remedy this supplies were bought almost exclusively from Milan. Milanese armour-making, which was in the control of one family, had mastered the art of making equipment tough enough to withstand a blow with a battle-axe; it could also be made to fit perfectly. (The skills of medieval armour-makers have not entirely disappeared nor are they entirely without application today. When the first spacemen's suits were made a few years ago, the armour repairers of the Tower of London, which houses a substantial museum, were approached for advice on complicated jointing problems – and were able to give it.)

However, by the end of the fourteenth century German craftsmen had succeeded in transferring this substantial industry to Nuremberg and Augsburg, and it will be noticed that many surviving suits of medieval armour are of German manufacture though of Italian design.

A further step towards humanizing the joust was the introduction of the tilt, a barrier placed between the two contestants so that their horses could not collide. This made the lance blows oblique and therefore more likely to glance off without serious injury. Armour was padded, but this was often more of a liability than an asset, and deaths from suffocation and heat-stroke were not unknown as a result. Exhaustion must have played a considerable part in the mock battle known as a *pas d'armes* or passage of arms. Here a team of holders (*tenans*) would hold a wooden castle or bridgehead against a team of attackers (*venans*). The contest went on from 1 p.m. till 7 p.m. for five weeks or more. There were elaborate rules, and beautiful women were the umpires, but it must have been a gruelling occasion.

Nowhere was the stratified nature of medieval life more clearly seen than in these knightly games. No one of inferior rank could participate, but with the social criterion satisfied there was no barrier of race, colour, creed, or even bastardy. In 1403 four Frenchmen fought four Spaniards at Valencia as a result of an obscure and trivial insult. Twelve years later, three Portuguese jousters lost a long and bitter contest with three Frenchmen at St Ouen and were booed from the lists, not because their cause was unpopular but because they were thought to have surrendered ungracefully! Bloody and barbaric though medieval life was, it maintained finer courtesies than much modern sport.

The tournament and joust lasted beyond the period with which we are concerned and were extremely popular in the sixteenth century. By that time armour and horse trappings had become enormously heavy, and although there was something to be said for these occasions as a spectacle, they lacked the skill, agility and courage that made medieval tournaments such exciting and dangerous pastimes.[1] An attempt was made to revive medieval glories in Ayrshire (Scotland) in 1839 as a result of the initiative of the Earl of Eglington. Ten thousand spectators arrived· to watch an impressive selection of home and foreign aristocracy disporting themselves in the lists, but the ultimate winner was the rain which fell intermittently throughout. Nevertheless, lances were broken and there was some excellent sword play in the evening under cover, notably by Prince Louis Napoleon. 1905 saw another revival at Brussels. This was more successful and more authentic in its details. There have been other lesser occasions, and as one occurred as recently as 1967 in England, there can be little doubt that there will be more.

Another form of entertainment which was occasionally available to the medieval castle-dweller was trial by combat. This was considerably more exciting than a visit to the law courts. It might involve a civil case, as when a man claimed that another was holding some part of his lawful heritage. Suits such as this were very frequent in the twelfth century, when few records existed and witnesses did not readily offer themselves lest they should themselves suffer a penalty. Some proof was needed for the claim to be accepted, but many defendants preferred a combat to a law case. Should either party fail to appear on the appointed day for a trial by combat

[1] Although accidents still happened, as when Henry II of France was killed in 1559.

he would be outlawed. The old and infirm were excused, as were clergy, but women were not, and occasionally, most discourteously, would gain the verdict. Men do not object to being prostrated by a woman's beauty but they find it extremely humiliating to be floored in physical combat.

In 1386 there was a notable duel in Paris between two French knights. Jean de Carouge had gone off on a Crusade leaving his young, beautiful, and, of course, virtuous wife in Argenteuil castle. Jacques de Gris, a trusted friend, appeared at Argenteuil one day and asked if he might be shown over their handsome home. He particularly requested to see the dungeon, and when she innocently conducted him there, suddenly locked the door and ravished her. When de Carouge returned from the Crusade she told him of what had happened in his absence, and he lost no time in applying to the King for permission to fight a duel to the death (*joûte à outrance*). The French King, Charles VI, was at Sluys at the time, organizing an invasion of England, but a *joûte à outrance* was too good a spectacle to miss, and he hurried back to act as umpire. The first stage, on horseback, went off without injury to either, but when they dismounted to fight with swords de Carouge sustained a serious wound in the thigh. In spite of this he continued the battle and soon obtained his revenge with a sword thrust through Le Gris's body. The latter died quickly but maintained his innocence of the accusation with his dying breath. Nevertheless, his body was given over to the common hangman and duly displayed on the gallows.

Some years afterwards another man made a deathbed confession to the crime. How the injured lady passed off this unfortunate discrepancy in her story is not recorded.

Our ancestors were always ready for a sporting spectacle, particularly if it included a fight, and they were not greatly concerned whether the fight was between the nobility, animals, or the lower classes, who were regarded in roughly that social priority. An interesting and popular sideline in Germany was – to judge from old woodcuts – fighting between man and wife. Occasionally the man would be handicapped, but if they were well-matched physically they would fight naked to the waist with short curved daggers. It was one way of severing the bonds of matrimony.

But whereas fighting was a highly prized diversion, sport, which meant the chase, was an overruling passion. The medieval addiction to sport may perhaps be compared to the modern craze for gambling. Nobody knows how many millions of pounds, and millions of man hours, are devoted to gambling fever today but few would attempt to deny that the quantity is gigantic. But medieval man was a compulsive gambler also. He took fantastic risks, usually staking his life in open warfare, or philosophically risking the loss of his head through engaging in a ridiculous and hopeless conspiracy in peacetime. Even the most level-headed of men were hopelessly addicted to suicidal risk-taking.

With the Normans, passion for the chase was second only to love of fighting. William I of England lost little time before introducing royal hunts in his newly-won territories. His best known achievement was to establish the New Forest in Hampshire as a royal hunting preserve, caring little that the deed uprooted a number of villagers and farmers who were then landless and homeless. But other forests were much larger. 'The whole of Essex lay under forest law, and the whole of the Midlands from Stamford Bridge in Lincolnshire south westwards to Oxford bridge, a distance of eighty miles. By the thirteenth century a great belt of forest extended from the Thames by Windsor through Berkshire and Hampshire to the south coast. The royal forest reached its greatest extent under Henry II, when it may have covered one-third of the country.'[1]

All the Norman kings of England were enthusiastic hunters. William I 'loved the tall deer' as if he had been their father' (although his way of showing his affection might not have appealed to everyone); William Rufus, the Conqueror's son, was so keen on hunting that he went out in spite of oracular warnings, and was killed by a chance arrow. Accidents of this kind usually occurred when the quarry turned and tried to break through the cordon of attackers. Men shot wildly, although it might be surmised that a few of the more malicious aimed more carefully than might have appeared. Henry I was jeeringly called 'hart's foot' – an obscure insult, on account of the family ruling passion, and Henry II was no exception to it. After Henry II the monarchy was of Angevin (Anjou) descent, and although still enthusiastic about the hunt, had not quite the passionate devotion of the Normans. Even so, the penalties for poaching were still severe – offenders were not only blinded but also castrated. Faced with these possibilities it was not surprising that poachers often chose to fight to the death with foresters and verderers, and not infrequently won.

Fashions in game change as do fashions in dress. The fox which is now a form of sanctified vermin was not even considered for the chase. Deer held pride of place (red, fallow, and roe), but wild boar (a very dangerous opponent) and wolves ran a good second. Wolf-hunting was not restricted, and in fact the heads of wolves were paid for. Wolves are said not to be interested in attacking humans; it is alleged that when they made dramatic and terrifying chases after sleighs in romantic fiction they were after the huskies and not the humans; however, this sort of information invariably

[1] Professor W.G. Hoskins, *The Making of the English Landscape*.

appears to emanate from laboratory-based scientists and not from people who made long journeys through a Europe infested with ravenous wolves. Certain areas of England had far too many wolves and the local lords had wolf-extermination as a duty of their manorial tenure. This task probably consisted less of exciting chases than digging out and killing the cubs.

The hare was valued both for sport and food. Unlike other animals it has the attractive habit of running in a circle, so if you do not catch it the first time round there is a chance on the second. Hares are also curious and have been known to follow a pack of beagles which are chasing a less fortunate neighbour. Rabbits did not appear in England till the thirteenth century, when they were introduced from France. Before the advent of the rabbit a warren was any place in which game was preserved, but subsequently appears to have changed its meaning. Fishing was also restricted in the royal forests, but fish were so plentiful that there was no real need to restrict their taking. Some legislation was introduced in the fourteenth century but this was mainly to prevent the waste of salmon. John Trevisa, writing at that time, said, 'The land is noble, copious, and rich of noble welles out of nobil ryveres with plenté of fische; there is great plenté of small fische, of samon, and of elys. So that cherles in som place fedith sowes with fische.' Salmon were, of course, so plentiful and cheap that there had to be laws protecting apprentices from being fed on nothing else; the statutory limit was twice a week.

In view of the popularity of hunting it is not surprising that dogs had a better time than many humans. Modern dogs are a poor copy of their sturdier ancestors, and many an animal that was once in the forefront of the chase has now been turned by the breeders into a wretched specimen which can hardly hold a sugared biscuit in its mouth without dropping it. Of the hounds, lymers and brachs hunted by scent (the latter was said to carry a good deal of its own); greyhounds, mastiffs and alaunts hunted by sight. Foxhounds in their modern form did not exist. A dog's life was a good life; it lived and ate with humans, it was not troubled by annual baths, and it followed its natural instincts. The more artistic hunters chose their hunting packs for the melody their blended calls could produce; this might not be everyone's idea of music but it was eminently satisfying to the lord of the manor. The yelp and yap of the hounds, the crashing through the greenwood, and the constant blast of the horn – the only means of keeping the chase together in woodland – must have made an impressive pandemonium.

The chase contributed considerably to the fact that castle fare was vastly superior to that available to – though not, perhaps, enjoyed by – inferiors. In the period under review, and for a considerable time afterwards, diet remained much the same; the only difference consisted in the way it was presented.

Bread, which was coarse and unattractive in appearance, was none the less vital. Just as corn had to be ground in the lord's mill (for a suitable fee), so bread had to be baked in a communal oven. These were usually built a few yards from the castle gates but in time of emergency would be moved inside. The official name for this factory oven was the 'four bannal', and the fact that everyone had to eat, and like, its product has given us the word 'banal' for commonplace. ('Bannock', with something of the same meaning, is Gaelic.) Doubtless many a housewife could have made better bread but was not allowed to do so.

In the castle every variety of bread would be found. The best quality, reserved for the lord and his family, was 'manchet', and was made of properly ground wheat but was coarse and discoloured for all that. Descending down the social scale we would find that some bread was made from coarse wheat flour but the bulk was made from rye. Outside the castle a form of bread would be made from peas or beans. This reliance on one basic cereal, rye, meant that bad or diseased crops hit rich and poor alike. It is now thought that the extraordinary occasions when whole districts went suddenly mad and started dancing as if possessed by devils was caused by ergot – a disease of rye.

Bread was not only vital to eat, it was also necessary to eat off. In this form it was known as a trencher, and about four days after baking made a workable plate. Sometimes one piece would be laid between two people who would place their meat on it when not gnawing. Forks were unknown and it was all hand-to-mouth work once the knife had severed the desired portion. A good trencherman would probably finish up the bread, but a less hungry or more generous man would hand it over to some poorer soul. As beggars wandered in and out of most halls, there was never any lack of outlet for charitable urges or even for bellows of rage.

Part of the function of bread was to mop up the extraordinary quantity of grease which was included in the cooking. Of these, the chief was lard. Numbers of cattle and sheep were killed and salted down in the autumn; many would be left for breeding purposes but the lack of winter feed would make them a sorry sight by spring. Pigs and chickens could fend for themselves, the pigs by eating beech mast, the fowls by eating worms and grubs. Of these two scavengers the pig was undoubtedly the more valuable, and the widespread use of the word 'larder' to this day shows how greatly he was valued for his by-products. Yet he had to wait

many years before anyone thought of making sausages out
of him.

But then, as now, most people were only too glad of any
excuse for a party. Whatever was eaten was always most
efficiently washed down with vast quantities of intoxicants,
if available. At the highest level this would be wine, but at all
levels beer would play a significant part. The Normans
imported wine on a heroic scale, perhaps because it was the
only way by which they could endure the British climate.
The Romans had also used wine for the same purpose. The
fact that English monarchs had French wives assisted them to
popularize wine drinking – not that it required much
assistance. Casualties in the Crusades were much increased by
the habit of keeping out the cold, fever, heat, disease and
homesickness by copious draughts of the local wines.
However destructive medieval armies were, they were seldom so foolish as to interfere with the activities of vineyards.
Vast quantities of wine were taken to war, particularly to
sieges. On more than one occasion we read that after the
castle well ran dry, flames were quenched with wine. Froissart
quotes an instance of two hundred shiploads of wine arriving
in England as early as the twelfth century. However, it seems
unlikely that these were the matured and mellow drinks we
enjoy today. This is not to underestimate the skill of the
vintners but merely to reflect that in the early days the
advantages of ageing were not appreciated. The fact that
wine and beer are so heavily taxed and highly priced today
has given rise to the idea that the tasks of brewing a decent
bottle of beer and making first-class wine are well beyond the
skill of the ordinary mortal; on the contrary, home brews are
often much superior to the medium-priced commercial
wines, and beers are sometimes as good as the best. There
was no social snobbery about drinking. Peasants drank wine

only if they were in vine-growing areas, otherwise they drank ale. Kings and nobles drank ale but, as it was produced without hops, must have found it a cloying beverage. It was also, probably, exceedingly strong. And as it was consumed in vast quantities there were undoubtedly massive hangovers.

As with food, our forbears were reluctant to leave anything in an unsophisticated state. Mead – which is simply brewed by fermenting honey and water – was blended with herbs to make metheglin. This, of course, was an old Saxon recipe. Cider made from apples would be blended with perry, made from pears; claret, by which is meant the wines of Bordeaux, was sweetened with honey and spices to make a potent liqueur known as hippocras, and any sweet wine was liable to be further sweetened and called malmsey, itself a general term for any sweet wine. But the finest skills went into the drinks we would now call punches. These were meant to preserve the teeth from decay and doubtless seemed to be doing so.

If we feel a little critical about medieval diet it is as well to remember that, whatever the dieticians and doctors say, 'a little of what you fancy does you good'. Possibly the good is mainly psychological. But our annual tribute to medieval feeding habits, the Christmas fare of pork and poultry – the only fresh meat available in their day – the dried fruit pudding which appears again in slightly altered form at tea as the cake, and at supper as the mince pies, does not seem to do anyone much harm; and if we took a quarter of the exercise our ancestors did, would not cause the slightest discomfort. Secondly, tributes to the medieval cook come at weddings, though the 'bride ale' is now champagne as often as not. Even so, the profusion of jellies, cakes, and other indigestibles, would warm the heart of a medieval caterer.

Medieval food has often been criticized for being over-prepared, over-seasoned, and over-coloured. All these charges may well be true, for it was roasted, boiled, mixed, mashed, baked, fried, and spiced; sometimes the same piece of food endured most of the foregoing processes. But oriental food gets something of the same treatment today, and though it may not preserve the vitamins it also fails to preserve other characteristics of food that is well past its best. When foods are kept they may ferment and produce a palatable drink like beer, or a pleasing taste like Gorgonzola cheese, or a chewable product like 'well-hung' venison, or a piquant flavour like 'ripe' pheasant, but if this process has gone too far (yet they are foods which cannot possibly be wasted), spices and ingenious cooking will make them eatable, digestible and nourishing. Unappetizing though the food may be when the cook first sets eyes on it, it still contains calories; if he can therefore put it into a form in which it can seem palatable, and is also digestible, he is a good cook.

It has been stated that the colouring of medieval food would repel us today, and it is difficult to refute this claim. But whether it would appear less attractive than modern food might do without the addition of colouring seems debatable. Perhaps we have become so used to seeing everything from meat to marzipan[1] tinctured that we could not face them without it. However, our wishes might fall short of liking to see it dyed red with blood, made yellow with saffron, or blackened with charcoal. Sanders, or saunders, a red dye made from sandalwood, was also very popular. Green was produced by boiling mint or parsley, and seems to have found particular favour for colouring pork! Curry is not mentioned, although, like scent, it must have been known to the Crusaders.

[1] Marzipan, originally 'marchpane' or 'massepain', was a great favourite in medieval times.

If we were reduced to a medieval diet today it would be vastly different from ours but not necessarily less interesting. Tea, coffee, sugar and some fruits would disappear, as would the potato. But in their place would be a variety of fresh food produced on the premises. Sea fish might be stale but not eggs, poultry or meat, river fish, vegetables or milk. Appetites would be less jaded than now and there would be honest pleasure in eating. Of course, the joy of plenty was only available to those who were rich, or attached to the rich.

Some of the dishes would be unfamiliar and not particularly palatable to modern tastes. Plover, goose, duck or pheasant would be appreciated, but not necessarily thrushes, finches and seagulls. Cormorant and vulture would be an acquired taste, but then so are certain cheeses. Perhaps one part of medieval cooking was to make the ingredients unidentifiable. Snake is swallowed more easily if it is assumed to be fish; monkey is decidedly less palatable if it is thought of as a near relation of the human race. Raw flesh is no problem if a man is hungry, or even if he is not and he thinks it contains vital rejuvenating vitamins. There are plenty of people alive today who have consumed uncivilized or decayed foods in wartime and are none the worse for it.

The engine-room of the castle was the kitchen. Without this, nothing could have functioned effectively. Some idea of its size may be gained from the Abbot's kitchen at Glastonbury, Somerset, England, or at Fontevrault Abbey near Saumur, France. Although built a little later than our period, the kitchen at Christ Church, Oxford (a college, not a church), gives a very fair example of how cooking was done in a large household. An impressive feature is the old table which is half a tree-trunk; one end is worn to the thickness of a plank by endless chopping, cutting, and grinding of food. But even today huge kitchens are strangely remote from everyday life. It is in comparison with cooking in bulk today that we should consider medieval cooking; roasting an ox whole was much the same then as now, and vastly different from doing a couple of chops under the grill.

One feature that distinguishes the medieval from the modern cook is his terminology. Blancmange is best paralleled by what today we call brawn, custard was what would now be called potted meat, and both might be served in 'coffins' which we should prefer to call flan cases. Fads were rife; certain foods which we should now consider beneficial and wholesome, such as fresh vegetables, were considered to be highly indigestible; others which we would regard as scarcely edible were considered to have vital, rejuvenating and aphrodisiac properties. Lampreys, which might well have described any eels, were a great favourite, and Henry I of England died of a surfeit of them, although his physician had many times warned him against this indulgence. But whether it was the food or the flies which covered it that accounted for many a premature medieval death is impossible to determine.

Presentation was important. The boar's head, with an orange in its mouth, is accepted still by all but the most squeamish. The pheasant, when redressed in its feathers is considered by some to be an attractive sight. But whether a roast swan, complete with long beak, plumage and feet, can ever have been a sight to whet the appetite seems debatable.

There was, it should be remembered, a sharp contrast between festive occasions and everyday diet. Perhaps the sharpness of the contrast made gluttony – when possible – so attractive. Breakfast would consist of bread, beer, and a little salt fish; dinner would be bread, beer, and a little salt meat. But there are plenty of nations today where breakfast consists of rice and salt fish, dinner of rice and stewed meat. Nor is it unusual for people to dip into the communal dish as they did in medieval Europe.

Mealtimes varied considerably from today's, and were also adjusted to the time of the year. Breakfast would be a snack taken on getting up; dinner would take place after four or five hours of daylight and might be at any time between half-past ten and noon. Supper would be at about 5 p.m., although it was not unknown for this to extend well into the evening as a drinking occasion. Dinner was the main meal of the day, and, in a castle where there might often be visitors, would be served with elaborate ceremony, often to an accompaniment of music.

Everyone carried his own knife which, at the end of the meal, would be wiped and returned to its sheath on the belt or girdle. As forks did not exist (though spoons did), hands became greasy. Hands were washed before and after the meal and this practice became something of a minor ceremony. Servants carried in water in ewers (sometimes called aqua-maniles), which were often elaborate representations of animals. The water poured over the hands was caught in bowls underneath. The ewer was replenished from a leather container known as a budget. (This container was found to be useful also for holding papers and accounts, and was soon used extensively by chancellors; the later significance survives in the 'budget statement' which the Chancellor of the Exchequer gives when introducing the Finance Bill in the English parliament.) Frequent wiping of the lips was necessary, particularly when the wine-cup was passed around, so the tablecloth would be used for this purpose.

From this era comes the word 'mess', now only used in the Services. A mess has nothing to do with the condition of the tables or floor but simply meant a meal, probably of meat, but perhaps deriving from *mettre*, through *mets*, to signify food placed on a table.

The hall of a castle, where every activity centred, varied considerably over the six hundred years with which we are concerned. In the early part of the period it would be a draughty, smoky hovel, with a hole in the roof, no proper ventilation, rushes on the floor, and a few rough oak tables down the middle. At one end there would be a raised portion where the lord and his immediate retinue would sit. Lighting would seldom be required, for men would tend to keep the same hours as the sunlight, but if illumination was needed it would be provided by smoky dips suspended over tallow. Such lamps are easily made but do not give much light. For certain occasions a torch could be kindled at the embers of the fire, which would stay hot all night in the castle. It was for lesser folk to obey the 'cure-feu', or curfew, that decreed they should cover their fires at a certain hour lest the flames should be fanned by a night breeze and perhaps set the whole township alight.

In later centuries the castle hall would become much more elaborate, and resemble the dining halls at Oxford and Cambridge Colleges and the Inns of Court today (see Appendix G).

There would be musicians' galleries, and tapestries on the walls. There would even be glass in the narrow, slit-like windows. There would be mural chambers in the walls which would give a modicum of privacy, not that it was much valued in a society where sleeping, eating, and love-making were happily conducted in public. The first and the last are now private matters; perhaps in a hundred years' time only uninhibited animals will be able to eat in public, for humans will be much too self-conscious.

Possibly this very public life was the reason why children,

both girls and boys, were sent away at a very early age to be brought up in other people's households; seven was the usual age. Perhaps it was thought that the child might not grow up to respect his parents if he saw too much of their diversions in his impressionable years. The custom is still carried on today where the boys, though not usually the girls, in a fairly well-to-do family are sent off to boarding schools far out of reach of sympathetic mothers and aunts, to learn to be manly – and, of course, do. But without a great weight of tradition it is unlikely that such a practice would continue.

And what were they not meant to see that everyone did but which would be unseemly in their own parents? The probable answer is some blatant love-affairs. Eleanor of Aquitaine was reputed to have had an affair with the Count of Anjou before she married his son, Henry II. Henry had an undiscriminating taste in women and produced one son from a common prostitute; the boy was made a bishop but was not an example of piety. Henry seduced the girl betrothed to his son Richard, and she bore him a child. Richard was a homosexual and perhaps did not care greatly, but is said to have fathered a few bastards himself. There must be a lot of royal blood in the community if we knew where to look for it.

But perhaps the medieval parent did not much care what his children saw. Children, as such, were a concept which did not exist. A person was either a helpless infant or someone who lived an adult life. According to Froissart, pages used to go round battlefields finishing off the wounded. Sometimes young lordlings were involved in the fighting and suffered for their father's sins. The Earl of Rutland, aged seventeen, was killed by Lord Clifford because the elder Rutland had killed the elder Clifford. Queen Margaret's son, at the age of seven, decided the form of death-sentences that should be inflicted on the captured Yorkists after the Battle of St Albans in 1461. Perhaps our precocious teenage delinquents are not so precocious or delinquent after all.

7

The Crusaders
and their Castles

The Crusades made an enormous impact on the techniques of castle-building and of medieval warfare. Because they took place far away, and there were so many threads and so many nations involved, the Crusades have been treated as something apart from the national history of contributor countries. Yet for three hundred and fifty years they diverted interest, energy, and resources. They also stimulated trade, brought about the prosperity of some and the ruin of others, and led to an interchange of ideas between East and West that would not have occurred otherwise for many years. They had a lasting influence on food, castle-building, architecture, furniture, and dress. There were in all eight main crusades, and a number of smaller expeditions which do not fully justify the title of crusade. There were also the hideous tragedies, mentioned earlier – the Children's Crusade and the expedition of Peter the Hermit.

By the end of the eleventh century Europe had settled down and stabilized. The great migration had stopped. Germany, although not yet homogeneous, was more than a collection of marauding tribes; England had been hammered into a unified country by the Norman conquerors; France no longer had to defend its frontiers against all comers; and the areas we now call Spain, Portugal, and Italy had an element of stability, if not of unity.

In the year 1095 the reasons for a crusade seemed very simple and uncomplicated. In the preceding three years the Middle Eastern emirates (local chieftains) had taken advantage of a weak Sultan to fight between themselves. This bickering had caused local anarchy and endangered the pilgrimages to Jerusalem, which were extremely popular. Pilgrimages, whether to the tombs of saints, healing waters, or memorials to great men, have always had a strong fascination, but the pilgrimage to the Holy Land has naturally been more compelling than any to Christians.

The responsibility for ensuring that the Holy Places were accessible to all who wished to go there seemed to fall naturally to the Pope. The Pope at that time was Urban II, and with Alexius Commenus, the Emperor of Byzantium, he initiated the First Crusade. Alexius was the military overlord, but as the Crusade was made up of a variety of different peoples it was not surprising that his command was little more than nominal. The field command was given to Raymond IV, Count of Toulouse, but as his divisional commanders included such independent characters as Duke Robert of Normandy (who spent his early life quarrelling with his father, and the latter part in being imprisoned by his brother), Godfrey of Bouillon – a man of fanatical individualism – and Bohemund of Apulia (an independent Norman duchy) it was not surprising that there was no coordination, no discipline, and little harmony. However, in spite of the lack of cohesion the Crusade took Jerusalem on 15 July 1099, and celebrated its restoration to the Christian faith by a massacre of Jews and Muslims that was said – and perhaps correctly – to have made the Holy Places run ankle-deep with blood. To consolidate this gain, Godfrey of Bouillon was made the first King, although his actual title was Defender. On his death his brother Baldwin succeeded, and was crowned on Christmas Day 1100.

However, the success of the military venture did not mean that any permanent security had been assured, or that access was any easier for the genuine pilgrims. Forty years later it was decided that another Crusade was necessary, and in 1147 two armies set out. Both were ambushed and the benefits to the pilgrims were negligible.

In the meantime, the Saracens were strengthening their hold on the area, and in October 1187 Saladin recaptured Jerusalem. This setback led to the best known of all Crusades – the Third. Its leaders were Richard Coeur-de-Lion of England, Philip Augustus of France, and Frederick Barbarossa, who enjoyed the titles of King of Germany and Holy Roman Emperor. Of these three glamorous characters, Barbarossa had the most impressive record. He was a fighter of such quality that for many years after his death it was believed that he would return like some military Messiah and lead his country to fresh triumphs. However, it is worth noting that when he besieged Milan he let himself in for later trouble which eventually led to his defeat by the Lombards in 1176. Possibly the ghost of Alboin, the King who had established the Lombards in Italy in the sixth century, was inspiring his opponents; Barbarossa's military record came to an abrupt end when he was drowned crossing a river at an early stage in the Crusade; he was sixty-five.

Richard Coeur-de-Lion and Philip Augustus distrusted each other so much that neither dared let the other venture alone; in consequence, they travelled together for most of the way. This arrangement did not stop Richard from calling at Cyprus where the ruler, who called himself 'Emperor' Commenus, had recently ill-treated some shipwrecked English sailors; Commenus was soon defeated and Richard celebrated his conquest of the island by marrying his fiancée, Berengaria of Navarre, in the church with considerable ceremony.

The Crusaders then proceeded to the Holy Land and after a considerable struggle captured the town of Acre. This was probably Richard's finest hour, for he was everywhere in the fight while his so-called ally, Philip Augustus, made none of the efforts of which he was undoubtedly capable. Richard added to his list of bitter enemies Leopold, Duke of Austria, who had rashly and without good reason placed his banner on the walls of Acre. Richard threw it into the ditch.

Philip Augustus then decided the moment was opportune to leave Richard in the lurch, so he sailed off giving the somewhat improbable assurance that he would not touch Richard's French territory while the latter was on a Crusade; on his arrival in France he lost no time in making appropriately treacherous arrangements with Richard's brother John, and the outcome was the need for Richard to build Château Gaillard. The end of that particular saga has already been described.

On this, as on all the other Crusades, the main handicap was ignorance of military geography, or for that matter of any accurate geography at all. Such plans as were made were based on fragmentary information from pilgrims and traders. Not surprisingly, the Crusaders sometimes found themselves attempting impossible or unsuitable tasks, like crossing the Armenian mountains. Pride of place for a feat of unnecessary endurance goes to Raymond of Toulouse, who took his army from Istria to Durazzo and lost half of it in the inhospitable territory of Dalmatia and Albania. On each expedition the Crusaders cherished the delusion that routes which had been used on a previous occasion would still be open; the Saracens had, of course, taken good care that they were not.

The only exception to this general misrouting occurred after the fall of Acre. Richard appreciated that a good part of the mountains of Ephraim lay between Acre and Jerusalem and therefore his best route would be down the coast road to Jaffa (Joppa), which he would use as a base and then strike inland. The eighty-mile march down the old Roman road would enable him to be supplied from the sea, which was just as well, as the Saracens had destroyed all potential supply points on his route. A Saracen eye-witness described the scene as follows:

The enemy moved in order of battle; their infantry marched between us and their cavalry, keeping as level and firm as a wall. Each foot-soldier had a thick cassock of felt, and under it a mail-shirt so strong that our arrows made no impression on them. They, meanwhile, shot at us with crossbows which struck down horse and man among the Moslems. I noted among them men who had from one to ten shafts sticking in their backs, yet trudged on at their ordinary pace and did not fall out of their ranks. . . . In the centre of their army there was visible a waggon carrying a tower as high as one of our minarets, on which was planted the king's banner . . . The Franks continued to advance in this order, fighting vigorously all the time; the Moslems sent in volleys of arrows from all sides, endeavouring to irritate the knights and to worry them into leaving their rampart of infantry. But it was all in vain; they kept their temper admirably and went on their way without hurrying themselves in the least, while their fleet sailed along the coast parallel with them till they reached their camping place for the night. It was impossible not to admire the patience which these people showed; they bore crushing fatigue though they had no proper military administration and were getting no personal advantage.

In the course of this gruelling march the Crusaders were able to defeat the Saracens in a sharp and bloody battle at

Arsouf (7 Sept. 1191). But it was of no permanent avail. Poor strategy and lack of support caused this Crusade to peter out like the others. Whatever Richard's faults – and they were numerous – his attempts to hold his motley army together were superb. He won the coastal towns but he failed in his objective of capturing Jerusalem and had to be content with making a three-year truce with Saladin which would give the pilgrims reasonable security. His bizarre journey home, when he was captured and kept in prison for a year, is a fascinating story but falls outside the scope of this book.

Within ten years the Fourth Crusade was launched on its remarkable and unpredicted path. Blessed by Pope Innocent III, the French barons had persuaded the Venetians to transport them, for the latter's fleet was widely renowned. Unfortunately, when the bill came in the French could not pay it. Not for nothing were the Venetians a people of great commercial drive so they suggested that the French should liquidate the debt by conquering Zara, a Dalmatian town held by the King of Hungary, and a prize much coveted by the Venetians. This was efficiently accomplished by the French, but while it paid the last bill made no provision for the next. The Venetians thoughtfully supplied the solution by hiring the Crusaders to attack Constantinople, which was then sacked and pillaged. Apart from being unutterably stupid and greedy, this deed was prejudicial to Western interests in that it weakened one of the bastions against the infidels.

The attack itself was, however, of considerable interest from the military point of view. The Crusader fleet moved in towards the walls under steady and accurate fire. The noise was said to be deafening. Both sides were using Greek fire in large quantities but both ships and city walls had been so well protected by wet hides that it could not take hold. Some damage was caused to the ships by missiles launched from the shore defences, but this was much less than might have been expected for the Crusaders had covered the more sensitive parts of their galleys with cushioning layers of brushwood. It seemed as if the main forces would not engage for a long time, if at all.

At this point the wind got up and blew half a gale towards the shore. The two leading craft, which had been lashed together to make a landing transport, were driven into and up on the beach. A few gusts later they were leaning over into the walls and wall towers. Fighting was desperate as both sides were well aware that there was no retreat for the attackers and it was a matter of kill or be killed. Meanwhile, other ships were being pushed up behind and nearby.

The day, of course, was far from lost, for a determined counter-attack by fresh troops, of which there were plenty, could have destroyed the assault party. But just away from the main battle a small probing party came across a gate which was little more than a postern and not as well defended. Once through this they were able to open a bigger gate and let in cavalry. Their effect was mainly on morale. Those manning the wall saw horsemen behind them and abandoned their positions. The city was not so much captured as thrown away.

The Fifth Crusade was equally abortive and misdirected, for it set itself the task of capturing Damietta in Egypt, in the expectation that the Saracens would then be happy to accept this city in exchange for Jerusalem. Damietta was eventually captured on 29 August 1219 after a seventeen-month-long siege (in which the Knights Templars saved the entire Christian army), but the Crusaders then unwisely decided to press on to further gains. A sudden Nile flood put a stop to

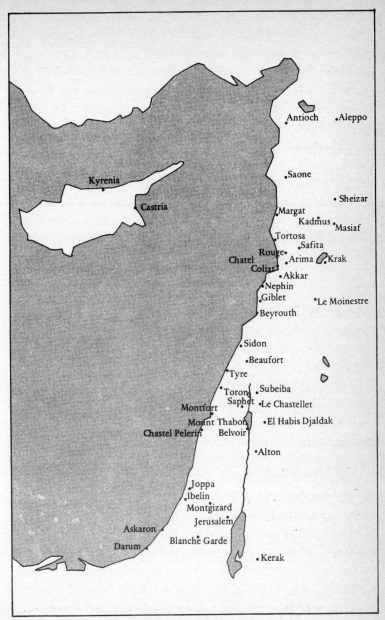

21   The location of Crusader castles in the Holy Land

their ambitions and made them only too happy to return Damietta in exchange for a safe conduct to Acre. The later Crusaders had no more success than the earlier. They established no permanent Christian settlement of the Holy Land. By the fourteenth century the Ottoman Turks had arrived, and they established an even firmer Muslim grip upon Palestine than the Seljukian Turks had done.

The Crusades might seem so extraordinary as to be almost a figment of imagination were it not for one durable souvenir, the Crusader castles. Even today these rugged buildings, which have endured extremes of temperature for nearly a thousand years, convey an intimidating effect.

As we have seen, the First Crusade began when the motte and bailey castles of the eleventh century were beginning to be replaced by stone erections. Where nowadays we would dig in, they built upwards; where we would try to blend into the landscape they would try to separate from and dominate it. A castle, it should be remembered, was a lookout position, and one would be the eyes and cover for another.

For Syria and Palestine, castles were ideal. The country they were required to hold was a long narrow strip, perhaps five hundred miles long by sixty wide. To the east lay powerful Saracen strongholds in the shape of Aleppo and Damascus. Both of these could have been captured relatively easily on the First Crusade, and again on the Third; after that, the opportunity was lost. The accompanying map (figure 21) should make this clear.

However, as we have already seen, the castles had more than one function. They were all-important storage depots and repair shops. And they were a substitute for numbers.

In these days, fire power is the reason for using smaller numbers; in those, fortifications served much the same purpose. Castles had the advantage to the holder that his numbers were difficult to gauge. Almost everyone in a castle was an 'effective'. A shower of quicklime hurts just as much whether it is poured down by a girl, an old man, or a doughty warrior. While besieging could be done by highly-trained troops only, defence could be undertaken by anyone, and usually was; there was no advantage in being a non-combatant in a situation which would probably end in men, women and children being butchered.

It was therefore vital to the Crusaders to build as soon as possible, and this they proceeded to do. The principles of siting remained the same as they had been elsewhere. Saphet was built in 1102 and seems to be the first of the Crusader castles. It covered the most northerly ford of the Jordan, and today is known as Safad. Toron (Tibnin) soon followed in 1116, to cover the road from Damascus to Tyre. Other castles belonging to this early period are Chastél Arnoul (El Burg), Scandelion (Iskanderun), Ile de Graye, and Saone (Sahyun), although the last of these was already in existence in a lesser form. The approach from Egypt was guarded by fortresses of Blanche Garde (Tel es Safi), Ibelin (Yibna) and Beth Gebelin.

Soon Beaufort (Kalat esh Shakif) joined them, as did Kerak of Moab and Krak des Chevaliers. Not all of these were held. Kerak of Moab, Montreal, Beaufort and Saphet were lost after epic and gruelling sieges; even so, they fulfilled part of their purpose, which was to exhaust the enemy. But as one set of defences fell so other, less impressive, fortifications were built to cope with the new situation thus created. Sometimes these were adaptations of Byzantine fortifications, and the blend of the Eastern style and the Western produced formidable and flexible structures. Hence we find that the Crusader castles served as prototypes for castles built in

Western Europe. The solid central keep was soon replaced by the massive gatehouse, area defence was organized through a pattern of mutually supporting fortifications, and the system of one castle drawing off attacks from its neighbour was mirrored in the system of one flanking tower covering another. Considerable thought was given to tactics before they were crystallized in stone. The principle of the ravelin, that is, a spearhead projection with fire-power on each side of the point, had been tried out by the Ancients; it was turned inside out as the barbican, but used in its original form outside the castle walls.

22   A view of Krak des Chevaliers, showing the concentric pattern and the flanking towers

Most famous, although neither the largest nor necessarily the most ingenious, of the Crusader castles is Krak des Chevaliers, or Kalat el Hosn, to give it its modern name. It lies in the Nusaïri mountains in southern Syria and has been considerably restored since 1927. Krak is built on a spur cut off from the rest of the rock by a deep ditch and looks as if it must have been impregnable, but in practice proved not to be so.

A site of such importance was probably fortified for centuries before the Crusaders arrived, but our knowledge of it begins between 1031 and 1142 when it was subjected to several brisk sieges. The earliest surviving portion is in the inner ward, and appears to have been built between 1140 and 1200. The defensive plan consists of two concentric lines of fortifications studded where necessary by powerful towers. The whole covers an area of about 150 by 225 metres, but these measurements give no conception of the grandeur of the setting, the vast galleries and halls, and the sheer beauty of archways, windows and roofs. Some idea of its capability may be gained from the fact that in its heyday it could accommodate six thousand people.

One useful military result of the Crusades was that castle design was fully tested. The European wars of the twelfth and thirteenth century saw very few occasions when a siege was resolved by military power alone. This point has been considered already, and due weight given to the influence of starvation and diversion. But in the Middle East, when attacks took place they were a military test from start to finish. The attackers were in no mood or logistical state to sit down and starve out a castle; their object was to destroy it. Such motivation produces an answering effect – concentration of killing power. The outcome was the concentric castle with a concentration of fire power which would settle the issue, one way or the other, in a remarkably short time. The unwelcome stranger at the gate would be greeted by a volley of missiles from the gatehouse, from three walls each topping the other, and from the nearby flanking towers. And this would only be the start of the invader's troubles. Each further step would involve him in a fresh set of disadvantages. However, as we have seen, most castles were eventually captured.

That the Crusades ended in failure is not a fact that is greatly lamented in European history books. Facile explanations are offered. The Crusades were impracticable, the contingents suffered from mutual jealousy and rivalry, the Crusaders made certain simple, excusable, but none the less disastrous, strategic and tactical errors. The fact that the Crusades took place a long way from home is offered as a suitable exoneration.

But certain facts stick out with embarrassing obviousness. If the strategists of the First Crusade had exercised rudimentary common-sense they would have captured Aleppo and Damascus and put several hundred miles of desert between the Saracens and their nearest base to the Holy Land. If, having failed in this first requirement, they had adequately supported the magnificent strategic concept of interlocking castle defence, there would have been no need for the waste and folly of the later expeditions. If, having captured territory, they had occupied it effectively, there would have been a more durable result for the two hundred years of conflict.

They had, of course, enormous handicaps. Not least was the fact of fighting a skilled and ruthless foe who did not hesitate to destroy everything in the path of the invaders; the fact that the Saracens had lived in the villages they burnt and had tended the crops they destroyed did not deter them for one moment in their 'scorched earth' policy. Consequently, the Crusaders were usually hungry, and often starving; their motley army with its horde of followers had neither the organization nor the supply train to cope with long journeys in barren lands.

An inevitable accompaniment of lack of geographical knowledge was complete ignorance of climate, where the land was bakingly hot in summer but could be flooded and bitterly cold in winter.

Last but not least of the factors which hindered them was their own arrogant stubbornness. Nobody took the trouble to learn any military lessons from predecessors, nobody made any attempt to organize a force in which the various arms were properly balanced. The fact that they left massive and imposing fixed defences in the shape of castles has created the impression that they were highly efficient militarily. They often fought successfully and sometimes campaigned brilliantly, but the final result of all their time, money, and effort, was to leave the situation for pilgrims considerably worse than it had been before the Crusades began.

One possible excuse for the failure of these massive fortifications to hold out the Saracen is the fact that they lost that essential quality of castles, their personal ownership. What is everybody's responsibility becomes all too easily nobody's. This is unimportant when matters are going fairly well, or even fairly badly, but when a need for desperation arises but personal property is not threatened there tends to be that lack of edge which makes the difference between victory and defeat. Certainly in all wars men tend to fight more fiercely for their homelands than for their principles.

This may perhaps seem an unfair criticism of the military brotherhoods to whom the task of defending the castles ultimately fell.

The Hospitallers and the Templars were both founded in the twelfth century. The Hospitallers (1113) were founded by merchants who, being on friendly terms with the Saracens, were able to obtain permission to establish a hospital for pilgrims who went to Jerusalem. It would be as much a hostel as a hospital, but it had the interesting addition to its Charter that its members would also take up arms in defence of the hospital, the Order, or the City. Originally, a hospital was an inn, a place for strangers or guests to be entertained, and a resting place. Soon it acquired the character of a refuge, and its doctors, who were often priests, were well aware that many ills require spiritual and mind healing as well as physical care. This reinforcement of the 'will to live', to get better, is now more than ever important in medicine. The Hospitallers at first wore old cast-off clothes but were not long in supplementing them with chain mail. Soon, the Order included in its ranks a number of wandering knights who were so appalled at their own records that they felt they must make an outstanding bid for forgiveness if they were not to spend eternity being roasted in hell. Having observed the discomfiture of some of their victims they preferred to expiate their own sins rather than pay for them. They fought extremely well when Jerusalem was occupied by hostile elements in 1191, but, being forced to leave, settled in Acre where they became the Knights of St John; later they were the Knights of Rhodes and then the Knights of Malta. Five years after the foundation of the Hospitallers another Order came into being, a military brotherhood dedicated to protecting pilgrims, fighting Saracens, and defending the Temple of Solomon in which they first lived. Not surprisingly, these became known as the Knights Templars.

In their early history these dedicated knights formed the garrisons in some of the castles we have mentioned. In the light of what has been said about lacking the ultimate incentive to hold on, it might be thought that they lacked courage, zeal, or skill; but this would be sadly wrong. Individually they were the bravest of the brave. They would fight to the death and never ask for terms, and as they never refused an engagement they were frequently held to their vows.

But being devout and brave is not necessarily the same as being successful. Virtue may bring its own reward but also perhaps its own downfall. The simplicity and worthiness of the Knights attracted huge legacies, and these in turn helped them to build up further resources. In time the Orders became rich, self-opinionated, and softened by luxury. They had always had their enemies but by the thirteenth century the accusations against them seem to have had some truth. At all events they were unable to hold off the Saracen challenge. Later the Orders declined further, and eventually disintegrated.

But while allotting to the Knights a share of the responsibility for losing the Crusader castles, their service to humanity should not be forgotten. A feature of medieval war which is seldom stressed is the fate of the wounded. Arrows inflicted agonizing wounds, and it needs little imagination to visualize the sufferings of a man crushed by a heavy stone. Many knights carried a 'misericord', a thin-bladed dagger which could be pushed through a crevice in armour to finish off a slowly-dying man; but the potential sufferer for whom it was carried was the owner. Unhappy the man who in his hour of irreparable agony had no friend to give him the *coup-de-grâce,* which was a stroke of mercy. The Knights Hospitallers introduced medical care to the battlefield and by skill and nursing restored to health many who would otherwise not have survived. When the scale of their resources is assessed it is not surprising that the Knights were widely renowned. Markab castle had a garrison of one thousand and was stocked for five years; Krak was said to be on twice the scale. It was a far cry from their original vows of poverty, chastity and obedience. Once they had dressed like peasants or beggars, but later some of their clothing was fit for princes.

There was never any doubt about the valour of the Templars, but their chastity and poverty seemed to be frailer commodities. Originally, many of them were Knights who had been excommunicated, and it was hardly surprising that in the heated moment there should have been subsequent lapses. Yet it was not ultimately their personal failings which caused their downfall, but their enormous wealth. The first two Knights Templars had only one horse between them, and the seal of the Order therefore depicted two men riding one horse. The Temple, off Fleet Street, London, is typical of the vast possessions they soon acquired, most of which were exempt from taxation. They had land all over Europe, complete with revenue-producing fairs and markets; the Paris Temple was the centre of the world money-market. To this day, many place-names commemorating the Order by the prefix 'Temple', as in Temple Balsall (Warwickshire). But as we have seen over and over again in history, ascetic orders founded by pious and dedicated men usually attract wealth, become corrupt, and are then suppressed by an impoverished monarch. This partly because they are corrupt but more usually because they have possessions which impecunious monarchs covet. The process may be assisted by some of those within the movement who think that a purge will clear the path for promotion. It does, but by the time it has finished few of the original actors are still on the stage.

A third Order of Knights developed from the German

23 Marienburg castle – now Malbork – was one of the strong castles of the Teutonic knights

contribution to the Crusades. This was the Order of the Teutonic Knights (1190), who did much to push German influence east, until like many before and after them they met their downfall through an overstretched line of communication.

This order had begun as an offshoot of the Hospitallers and therefore was dedicated to the care of the sick and the needy, but had also adopted the military attitudes of the Templars.

It saw as its mission the conversion of all the heathen to the north-east of Germany. As this generic description covered Prussians, Letts, Wends and Slavs, it is clear that they were not short of tasks. As they pushed back the frontiers of Germany, the traders followed them; they crossed the Oder and laid the foundation for Prussia by the establishment of military border states. One of these was Brandenburg. Eventually the Knights were defeated in a shattering battle at Tannenberg in 1410, when a combined Polish and Lithuanian force proved too good for the heroic Order, whose commander-in-chief was killed. From then on the influence of the Teutonic knights declined.

But during the century and half in which they were in the ascendant the Teutonic knights built a number of unusual, interesting, and often beautiful, castles. Their ideals determined that their castles must be a combination of monastery and fortress; in consequence, the principal architectural form was a square made up of four functional blocks, chapel, dormitory, refectory and hospital. Some of the earlier castles were unable to take this characteristic form, for military necessity demanded that they should be superimposed on earlier fortresses of a somewhat different design. But this form was used as early as 1280 at Marienburg and Lochstedt, and before the end of the century by Rheden and Mewe. In order to make this type of building more defensible, flanking towers were added and the front was usually protected by a barbican; sometimes there would be an outer wall enclosing other external buildings, and this would create an outer bailey and give the whole structure a concentric form. The most impressive of all their castles was Marienburg in West Prussia, which was the seat of the High Master. The interior of this building contained rooms with delicate fan-vaulting and pillars in the most elegant Gothic tradition. (The

Master's refectory was described as 'music turned to stone'.)

Closely linked to and resembling the castles were the Bishops' palaces. Buildings such as Marienwerder in West Prussia, Heilsberg in East Prussia, and Arensburg in Estonia, were less formidable than the true castles but were not to be underrated militarily nevertheless. The Teutonic Knights never lost sight of their military function. They were in constant rivalry with the Church, with the local people who resented their presence, and with the Hanseatic League. And there was always an element of danger from the presence of the nearby Russians. On the one side of the river Narva stood the Russian border fort Ivangorod, and on the other was Hermannsburg which had been considerably strengthened since it had been taken over from the Danes. In the fourteenth century these symbolized military and ideological rivalry as clearly as the two halves of Berlin do today.

8

Thirteenth-century Castles and the Factors which influenced their Design

By the middle of the thirteenth century European castles settled into forms which showed that the period of evolution was virtually over, and that future castles would merely be improvements or adaptations of existing patterns. The most striking of these were the concentric castles, which showed the Byzantine influence brought home by the Crusaders, but it was clear that other less complicated styles would have a continuing use. At the end of the century Edward I was building highly sophisticated fortresses in Wales, but a hundred years later the Scots were still finding that the best building for their purposes was a square keep or tower-house, solid, uncomplicated, but extremely formidable. By the end of the fifteenth century it was widely believed that the day of the castle was over, that gunpowder had put an end to this type of fortification, that in the future battles would be decided in the open field, and that the only possible use for a castle was to make it into a comfortable though indefensible residence. But as we have already seen, the castle, at all stages in its career, had a way of being unpredictable, and never was this more clearly shown than when its day was popularly believed to be over. Even so, few would dispute that medieval fortification was at its peak in the fourteenth century. Among the finest castles ever built were the highly expensive series produced for Edward I after his conquest of Wales. Their cost, strength and disposition are a great tribute to the fighting qualities of the Welsh people.

The Welsh, of course, are born warriors, and although a hospitable people, seldom extend anything but a military welcome to the invader. The exception is when a known neighbour is hated more than an unknown newcomer, and on such occasions it would be possible for the English to make an alliance with one of two deadly enemies. There was no need to divide and rule; the Welsh were already divided. Living in remote valleys, cut off from their neighbours by hill country which made social contacts difficult but military forays easy, it was hardly surprising that they were dis-united. And where life is hard and food is scarce, a man tends to guard his own and covet his neighbour's.

When Edward I came to the English throne he had clear ideas about his rights and ambitions. In brief, his programme was to conquer Wales, conquer Scotland, and conquer France. The Welsh came first on his agenda because they were too great a menace to be left on his flank while he stretched his line to Scotland.

There was on hand a vast quantity of military intelligence on the Welsh and their country. The Romans had subdued the inhabitants of South Wales, whom they knew as the Silurians, and administered this territory from Caerleon-on-Usk; but the Ordovices, who inhabited the mountainous

north, were not conquered but merely kept in check by the
Chester garrison. The difference was one of terrain, not of
fighting qualities. The south offered certain valleys and rivers
which helped the invader to penetrate, but the north was a
tangle of mountains, steep, foggy, wet, and occasionally
marshy. In this setting the Welsh, who lived off meat, milk,
butter and cheese, from cattle, sheep or goats, had a degree of
mobility which no would-be conqueror could equal. All the
former needed to do was to retreat into the hills, lead on the
wretched invader till he was dropping from exhaustion, cut
off his retreat, and harass him with guerilla raids; a pitched
battle would be unnecessary and unwise. However, on a
number of occasions the Welsh did launch themselves into
pitched battles, sometimes scarcely armed. As Giraldus
Cambrensis put it, 'when the trumpet sounds the alarm the
husbandman rushes as eagerly from the plough as the courtier
from the court; they deem it a disgrace to die in bed, an
honour to die in the field of battle'. One of the latter occasions
had happened in Henry II's reign. The English King had
assembled a mixed mercenary force from England, Normandy, Flanders, Anjou and Gascony, and advanced into the
Ceirog valley. The Welsh assembled the largest force available and confronted the invader. For a short time there was
no action, for Henry made a temporary wooden fort while
the Welsh skirmished around. After a while, some of the
Welsh became impatient and hurled themselves on the
English King's force. The ensuing battle was fought with
such desperation that the site (Crogen) gave a new word
to the language, and for centuries described a battle or fighter
of desperate courage. In consequence, Henry's expedition
failed.

As we have already mentioned, the Norman theory of
government was to pin down a country with castles whose

owners had a personal stake in the land they occupied. After the initial share-out of the English Kingdom in 1066 there was little left for rewarding later supporters of the Norman cause. The answer to the problem came from Wales, Scotland and Ireland. Not least of the attractions of these territories was that any acquisition would be preceded by long and arduous campaigns; the Normans, like most of their opponents, were never happier than when in the middle of a fight. But attempts to conquer Wales as a whole did not succeed, although invasion forces often penetrated as far as Snowdon. And there was the age-old problem that the settler often became fonder of his new friends than his old ones. Moreover, border lords were inclined to carve out an independent existence and treat their English king with scorn, perhaps even rebel against him. When they did so they had to be subdued, and when the subjugation had taken place a gap was left that could not be easily filled. Robert of Belesme, Earl of Shrewsbury, is a case in point. If he could have behaved himself he would have made a splendid bulwark and spearhead for Norman policy against Wales. Instead, he chose to be too independent, and after his fall even his brother Arnulf of Montgomery, who was in Cardigan, had to be removed. Good though this was for discipline, it left a gap which took centuries to fill.

Up in the north fighting was almost continuous. Rhuddlan changed hands on a number of occasions, as did Deganwy, opposite Conway. The main area of conflict was the Four Cantreds (a cantred was an administrative district) between the Dee and the Conway; these saw most of the bloodshed. The main bases for the English were Shrewsbury and Chester. In front of them was a defensive fan of castles such as Mold, Hawarden, Oswestry and Ludlow, to name only some. Before Edward I, North Wales had been a delightful play-

ground for the belligerently minded, and had even been the
subject of deep military thought, but no one had overcome
the problem of holding territory once it was overrun. Some
of the invaders – Henry II was one – had been washed away
by rain. It was an irritating situation because in the south the
position was stable and the Marcher Lords,[1] as they were
called, were now integrated by marriage, might, or passive
acceptance, with the native peoples. But the northern
fastness of Gwynedd remained as Welsh as its name.

In the year 1272, when Edward I came to the English
throne, a similarly powerful character, Llewellyn, had taken
over the Principality of Gwynedd. For the moment North
Wales was united, but Edward was not perturbed provided
Llewellyn did the appropriate homage. But Llewellyn not
only refused to do homage but allied himself with the
French. Furthermore, he proposed to take a bride from the
French court, a lady called Eleanor de Montfort, daughter of
the rebel Earl who had kept Edward and his father prisoner
but a few years before. Unluckily for her but fortuitously for
Edward, she was captured by a Bristol merchantman when
she was on her way to join Llewellyn. With this prize in his
hands Edward once more invited Llewellyn to do homage;
but even now was refused. Clearly it was the time for action,
not words, and in a short time a vast army had invaded Wales
and blockaded every entrance and egress. With overwhelming defeat staring him in the face, Llewellyn had little
alternative but to do the required homage. Apart from this,
the terms were surprisingly mild. He was united to his bride
and treated with great kindness and courtesy.

But passions and pride were running too high for this
matter to be settled without a fight to the finish. As Edward

---

[1] Central and Southern Wales were known as the Marches, a word denoting contestable
frontier country.

pressed on with the anglicization of Welsh laws and ways, Llewellyn sat back and watched. Then with supreme timing he made a bid for Welsh independence, or committed an act of foul treachery, according to which side your sympathies lay. In 1282 he and his brother issued a call to arms, launched an undeclared war, and killed and burnt everyone and everything English they could lay their hands on in North Wales.

Edward was not a man to make a mistake twice. This would be the second, but the last time. He assembled a powerful army and a fleet to match it. Confronted with this gesture of power most of the Welsh realized that further resistance was useless. Llewellyn was swiftly driven back to Snowdon, and once more asked for terms. But Edward was resolved not to be fooled again. The peace conditions were harsh. Llewellyn should leave Wales for ever and become an English earl. Gwynedd would cease to exist.

It could have been a desperate situation involving gruelling fights to the finish but it was resolved unexpectedly; Llewellyn was killed in a skirmish by an esquire[1] who did not know whom he was fighting. Resistance would of course continue, but it was unlikely to be on the same scale again. At least, that was what men thought.

There was now nothing to stop Edward carrying out his policy for Wales, and every reason for him to press on with it regardless of expense. Gwynedd was abolished; in its place were created the three districts of Anglesey, Merioneth, and Caernarvon. The next stage was to build a system of roads and castles so that every vital point could be reached and every key strategic centre would be under English control.

Although the best known of Edward's Welsh castles are Conway, Caernarvon, Harlech and Beaumaris, these are by

[1] Adam of Frankton.

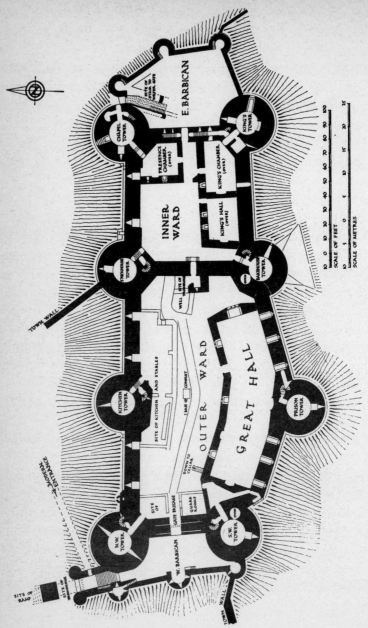

24   Ground plan of Conway castle

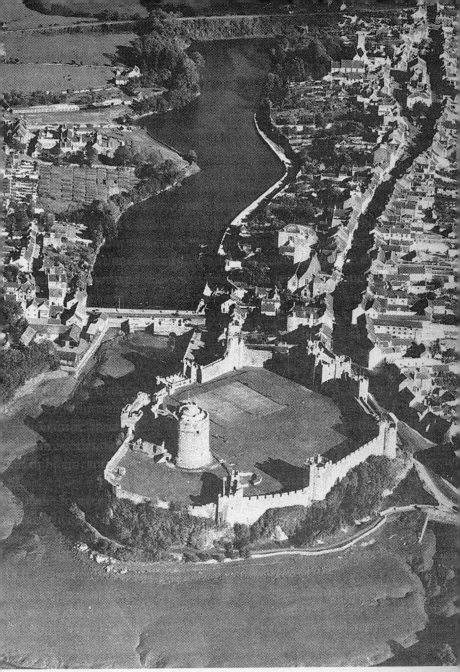

25 Pembroke. A castle guarding the mouth of a river. The keep was
built in the late twelfth century and is 100 foot high; it has no
buttresses, arcading or vaulting. It is roofed with a stone dome, and
the walls are nineteen feet thick at the base. Similar – though not
identical – keeps were built at Coucy and Bothwell

no means the total of his efforts. In 1277 he completely
rebuilt Flint, Aberystwyth, Rhuddlan and Builth. Unfortunately, no masonry remains on the massive earthworks
of Builth to tell what it once was, but its military record – a
central Wales castle which was never captured – is convincing
enough. The other three had the great advantage that they
could be supplied from the sea, although for Rhuddlan this
meant diverting a river from its former course. And there
were others which were reconstructed, strengthened, or
linked into a defensive network.

But as examples of military engineering, Conway,
Caernarvon, Harlech and Beaumaris represent an outstanding achievement. Harlech and Beaumaris are beautifully
proportioned and sited concentric castles; Conway and
Caernarvon are linear defences because of their sites, which
made this form of design necessary. However, in their
situations Conway and Caernarvon are no less formidable
than the others.

To begin with Conway. Fourteen years ago the Ministry
of Works estimated that at that time the comparative cost
was about £1,500,000. The time it took was approximately
nine years, although of course with a building of that size and
nature, alterations, modifications and repairs would always
be going on; at Conway, repairs to keep it on a war footing
were still being carried on in 1645, nearly three hundred and
fifty years later.

In previous centuries castles had dominated and overawed
towns; in this era the castle took the town into its perimeter
walls and protected it. Conway town and castle are situated
on a triangle of rock, with the castle at the top of the triangle
pointing towards the water. The curtain wall is high and is
studded with twenty-eight towers all of which are open on
the inside, so that any attacker who broke through at this

point would be exposed to fire from the interior. There were three gates and a postern, the latter opening on to the seashore. Each of the gates was heavily protected by flanking towers, portcullises and a drawbridge. The castle itself was heavily defended at each end by barbicans, and its eight powerful drum towers were so spaced as to cover and protect each other precisely. Clearly this would be a place to defy all but the most powerful attack; this interdependence of town and castle had been growing up in other areas, but Conway was the first place to design it into the overall structure.

To describe castles like Conway in prose may be compared with writing about famous paintings. The size, proportions and colouring may be defined easily and accurately, but the reader is still left without any real conception of the achievement. As many castles are now in ruins, and they were originally meant for function and not for beauty, they draw less admiration than cathedrals or churches, which are usually well preserved. Conway goes a considerable way to redress the balance; although but a shadow of its former magnificence it still conveys an impression of power and beauty, which can neither be comprehended nor appreciated without seeing.

Two remarkable feats of archery belong to this area. One of them relates to the Wars of the Roses when the Yorkists held Conway (in the year 1461). The Lancastrians were observing the castle from Tal-y-sarnau on the other side of the river, about half-a-mile away. A Yorkist archer, who bore the resounding name of Llewellyn of Nannau, transfixed a Lancastrian. Clearly there was a large element of luck in such a shot; the victim was probably standing in a group and was one of several who could have been hit. The distance was approximately twice the normal crossbow range.

In the early years of the present century Sir Ralph Payne-Gallwey, who built and tested medieval weapons from longbows to trebuchets, fired several crossbow bolts across the Menai Straits – a distance of 450 yards. The weapon he used was a fifteenth-century steel crossbow.

The second great Edwardian castle to be built on linear lines was Caernarvon, and this, although not necessarily more impressive than Conway, is perhaps more elegant. Even today it is rated more as a palace than a castle.

Strategically, Caernarvon commands the southern end of the Menai Straits, but Edward decided it should have more than a military function. His son Edward was born there, and

26   Caerphilly castle. A formidable Welsh thirteenth-century castle whose impregnability came from the damming of a small stream. The 'leaning tower' (*bottom left*) of the Inner Ward was blown up by Cromwellian forces at the end of the Civil War (1649); it has leaned perilously for three hundred years

was named Prince of Wales; however, at the time the ill-fated Edward II was not the eldest son and it did not seem over-likely that he would ever succeed to the English throne. Subsequently the idea of the eldest son of the English monarch being the hereditary ruler of Wales has been sedulously fostered, and in 1968 Charles, Prince of Wales, was cere-monially invested at Caernarvon.

Like Conway, Caernarvon was master-minded by James of St George, an architect of international repute from Savoy. Others scarcely less capable succeeded him for the later stages. There was a setback in 1294, eleven years after the castle's inception, when Prince Madog, son of the last Prince Llewellyn, raised a rebellion and burnt a good part of the buildings. He may have had good reason to make a special point of Caernarvon for it is heavily rumoured that when Prince Llewellyn had been killed Edward I had his head served up on a dish at a banquet at Conway or Caernarvon; not, we hasten to add, because he was a cannibal but because he thought that the news would make suitable impression on the Welsh. It did, but not in the way he intended.

Caernarvon castle is shaped like an hour-glass and lies along the bottom line of a large D-shaped wall, which enclosed the original town. As at Conway the outer wall is studded with defensive towers, all of which are open on the inside. But the beauty of Caernarvon is the variety of angles from which arrows and missiles could be launched. As the nerve-centre of Edward's command of Wales it was meant to be a symbol, and anyone who sees it today, nearly seven hundred years after the first trench was dug and first stone laid, cannot but feel that building is an art in which little real progress has been made. The fact that for four centuries this castle was neglected, plundered and allowed to fall into ruins, seems scarcely credible; what modern building could survive

27 Beaumaris. The moated outer ward shows how arrow loops in flanking towers gave a field of fire along the wall

such treatment after such a span of time?

But the most efficient of the Edwardian Welsh castles are the concentric ones, of which Beaumaris and Harlech are most famous. Beaumaris is on the island of Anglesey, which was the granary of Wales. No rebellion could therefore hope for any success unless it began by capturing this coastal castle.

It has the neatest of designs. Again it was James of St George who designed the plan, this time without the site imposing any restrictions. In consequence, we find a simple but completely effective pattern. The inner ward is rectangular with a tower at each corner, and a tower in the centre of the east and west walls. In the centre of the north and south walls there is a gallery defended by two barbican-type towers. The outer ward was octagonal, and again was heavily defended by towers at every point where a tower might be of use. But the great feature of castle defence was the one mentioned earlier – to make a series of 'killing grounds' where the unwelcome would be destroyed. At Beaumaris these were provided by the narrowness of the interior of the outer ward, which made it impossible to concentrate a force large enough to storm the inner walls. Furthermore, the gateways in the outer wall are slightly to the left of the gatehouses in the inner ward; anyone fortunate – or unfortunate – enough to break through the outer gate would have to turn at right angles and approach the inner gate obliquely from the left. Apart from the physical disadvantage of approaching an enemy by manoeuvring to the right there seems to be a psychological factor, as any boxer who faces a 'southpaw' will know.

Concentric design had the enormous advantage over linear defence that it could concentrate the fire from several defensive lines on to one attacker. This was clearly so at Beaumaris where the approacher was raked by fire from in front, from above, and from each side. And all this while he was negotiating the moat.

Beaumaris – 'the beautiful marsh' – is aptly named. It has the beauty of a sharp sword, an impressive but slightly awesome sight; only in the interior does the appearance become mellow, where the chapel and its living quarters suggest that men occasionally thought of matters other than mutual

28 Harlech castle. The castle which stood a seven year siege

destruction (within those fifty-feet-high, sixteen-feet-thick walls).

But the functional life of Beaumaris was short; it had been allowed to fall into disrepair by the next reign.

As we have seen, military controversy is the most consistent matter in warfare. Few doubts assailed the minds of those who believed that longbows were better than crossbows, that infantrymen were a greater asset than cavalrymen, that aircraft were more valuable than submarines, and that these tactics were better than those. Particularly is this controversy keen when it is necessary to make a virtue out of a necessity. When there was water, a wet moat was the best; if not, there was nothing, nothing at all, to match a dry ditch. Where there was a suitable rocky eminence, that was the ideal castle site; but where the land was low-lying and marshy, like Beaumaris, its value was unquestionable. Harlech, which was on a headland set above a marshy plain, seems to have been fortunate in combining the best of both worlds, though doubtless it had its contemporary critics.

Harlech is concentric, but of a simpler design than Beaumaris. The central ward is rectangular but has only one gatehouse; however, this gatehouse is a castle in itself. There were probably two problems in the mind of the architect when he planned this gatehouse; one was the possibility of surprise by the ever-resourceful Welsh, who might well find a way through the outer ward; the other was the need for the castellan to have a retreat from any rebellious activities by his own garrison. The latter problem became particularly troublesome during the second half of the fourteenth century, when the castles were full of soldiers whose concept of military life was continuous destructive activity whether in war or peace – a habit they had picked up in the French wars. Strictly speaking, 'livery and maintenance' meant providing food and lodging for retainers, but in practice it also meant keeping a watchful eye on a turbulent, quarrelsome, excitable garrison of veteran soldiers who, like many garrison troops before and after, were liable to disperse boredom by mutiny. In the absence of cinema shows, current affairs talks, paperbacks, and similar comforts for the troops, the only way to keep soldiers out of mischief was to practise them at arms drill till they dropped, and to let them loose on the surrounding countryside when they were too tired to do much harm. And it was not merely snobbery which kept the officers' quarters apart and 'off limits to troops'; it was simple recognition of the fact that anyone but a known servant who was found in certain parts of the castle was not there to preserve good order and military discipline.

The cost, financing, labour and speed of construction of the Edwardian castles may be obtained from contemporary accounts although, unfortunately, these are not complete. However, there is enough information available for us to gauge the size, complexity and difficulties of the enterprise.

Aberystwyth, Flint, Rhuddlan, Conway and Caernarvon took the adjoining towns into their system of fortification and therefore the expenditure at these sites included a long curtain wall equipped with formidable towers and defensible gateways. Conway provides the best example of a strong town wall; and it is still possible to walk along much of it today. If we compare wages at that time, i.e. masons at 4d a day, and semi-skilled diggers and rock-cutters at 2d a day, with present-day wages we can obtain a rough guide to the outlay involved. There were, of course, plenty of other types of work and workmen, whose activities are less easily compared. However, it is unlikely that the above castles and walls cost much less than £3 million each (in present-day values) when the total costs are set out. As we see later, there were many hidden or intangible costs, and the figure quoted might well be an underestimate.

Builth, Beaumaris and Harlech would have cost less than the others because they were smaller, but it is easy to underestimate the total outlay involved unless we pay very careful attention to the difficulties of building on those sites. Certainly no expense was spared to make them impregnable. This is very noticeable if the visitor goes from one to the other; no matter which one he finds himself in, he always feels it must have been ideal for its purpose.

The costs which are usually omitted from estimates of expenditure on the Edwardian Welsh castles were of transporting and paying workmen from all over England, and, for some highly-skilled men, from distant parts of Europe. As regards the former, the records for the year 1277 show the following:

Three hundred carpenters from Derbyshire.

Three hundred ditch-diggers from Yorkshire.

One hundred and twenty carpenters from Wiltshire.

One hundred and twenty masons from Dorset.

One hundred carpenters from Leicestershire.

Similar lists may be compiled for following years but the figures do not appear in the building accounts because they were paid by the sheriff of the workmen's home shires. They represent a fraction of the total number employed. A report states that in 1296 at Beaumaris four hundred masons were at work cutting and laying stone, assisted by one thousand mortar-and-lime mixers, two hundred carters and thirty smiths and carpenters. As the Welsh were only too ready to disrupt these activities, a force of one hundred and thirty soldiers, including twenty crossbowmen, were there to frustrate their efforts, and very necessary they were.

Contemporary documents mention a number of complaints about arrears of wages, and rivalry between one site and another which caused essential supplies to be diverted from their original destination. Work often fell behind schedule. Building, in the British Isles, is a seasonal activity, and during five winter months operations would be drastically reduced if not stopped altogether; exceptional bad weather conditions could further curtail activities.

Needless to say, this vast enterprise could not have been financed from money raised in conquered Wales. Half of the payments came from royal 'wardrobe' accounts, the remainder were met from Irish revenues. The Irish would doubtless have resented paying for castles in Wales nearly as much as the Welsh disliked seeing them built. In the Sir John Rhys Memorial lecture which he gave to the British Academy in 1944, J.Goronwy Edwards gave the following figures as the recorded expenditure on Welsh castles up till the year 1301, stressing that they probably fell about £14,000 short of the final figure:

Builth (1277–82): £1,666 9s. 5¼d.

Harlech (1285–92): £8,184 10s. 9d. (plus unknown amounts in the seasons of 1283, 1284, 1291).

Beaumaris (1295–8): £11,289 0s. 9d. (a further £1,547 12s. 11¾d. was spent between 1309 and 1323).

Aberystwyth (1277–89): £3,888 17s. 11½d. (plus unknown amounts for rebuilding after 1282 when it was destroyed and burnt by the Welsh).

Flint (1277–86): £7,021 13s. 7¾d.

Rhuddlan (1277–85): £9,505 15s. 9¼d. (including £755 5s. 3d. on making the channel to the sea).

Conway (1283–92): £13,689 15s. 6½d. (plus unknown amounts in the seasons of 1283–4, 1290, and 1291).

Caernarvon (1284–1301): £12,285 18s. 7¼d. (plus unknown amounts in 1283–4, 1291, 1293–4, and a known amount of £3,497 14s. 11½d. between 1304 and 1323).

Standing on the battlements or towers of these castles it is easy to appreciate the skill of the siter, the architect, and the mason, but there were other contributors to these castles whose work was no less important. Among them was Master Manasser from Vaucouleurs in Champagne, who directed the digging operations. As these involved hewing moats and foundations out of the solid rock without the aid of modern tools, the talent of the workers was not inconsiderable.

Although Edward was able to leave his mark on Wales he was less successful in Scotland, and was content to maintain the *status quo* in Ireland. Over in France he made some claim to be regarded as much as a diplomat as a soldier. However, it would be unfair to Wales to imply that he found it an easier task than Scotland; both were worthy opponents of a man who has good claim to be regarded as one of the greatest of fighting kings.

Had fate been less cruel Edward would never have needed to have fought the Scots at all. But in 1286 the last king of the Canmore line was carried over the cliffs of Kinghorn by an over-spirited horse. His granddaughter and heir, a child of four, was in Norway at the time, and stayed there while a Regency ruled Scotland on her behalf. When she was seven it seemed a splendid idea that she should be brought home and married to Edward I's son, the Prince of Wales. And indeed, if it had come to pass, this marriage would certainly have saved much futile bloodshed and the murder of Edward II. But, alas for hopes, 'the Maid of Norway' was tossed around the North Sea for six weeks in unprecedented autumn storms and died soon after landing. The union of England, Wales and Scotland was postponed for four centuries.

Ironically, the fact that Edward was asked to decide

between the rival claimants to the Scottish throne eventually brought him to war with Scotland. After much deliberation he chose John Balliol instead of Robert Bruce, and expected his choice to do feudal homage. As he was himself repudiating the feudal homage the King of France expected from him as holder of the Dukedom of Aquitaine, it was not surprising that the Scottish barons refused to allow the weak Balliol to supply this token of subservience. Edward could not present his point of view until he had dealt with Madog's rebellion in Wales, but by 1296 he was ready; he captured Berwick, then the chief port of Scotland, and followed this gain by hammering the Scots at Dunbar. Then he turned his attention to France.

But Dunbar was the first, not the last, round of this conflict. Soon the Scots were up in arms under William Wallace and turned the tables on the English at Stirling (1297).

By 1298 Edward's hands were sufficiently free of his continental troubles for him to give his attention to Scotland again, and by 1304 it seemed as though that country was destined for the same fate as Gwynedd.

In 1306 events took an unexpected turn with the advent of another Robert Bruce, grandson of the man who had formerly competed with Balliol for the Scottish throne. Bruce's record was far from savoury but he attracted a large following and had a number of spectacular successes. In consequence, Edward pursued a policy of unstinted cruelty and ruthlessness with the intention of frightening the Scots away from allegiance to their new hero. But policies of this kind harden resistance rather than disperse it. Men who had had their land confiscated joined Bruce in large numbers, and by 1307 the Scot had a formidable army of desperate veterans.

Once more Edward took the field, but this time as an old

man with failing health. In July 1307 the 'hammer of the Scots' slipped out of the saddle for the last time, and four days later was dead. His son, although sworn to pursue his father's policies, and even to carrying his bones with the army to frighten the Scots, broke off the engagement and returned to London. Although pressure of English opinion would make Edward II return to Scotland with an army seven years later, it would only result in the disastrous defeat of Bannockburn. The Scots had won what they subsequently called their 'Wars of Independence'. Unfortunately, the bitterness bred in this conflict ended a reasonably peaceable relationship between the two countries and set the stage for three hundred years of bloody war and skirmishing.

The effect of these historical events is marked by phases of castle-building. Like many other countries, Scotland carries traces of fortifications and towers which date back to pre-Christian times. Some of these may well have been built by invaders; certainly, at a much later date, the Norwegians built a stone castle in the Orkneys which they then owned. The Normans did not, as we know, conquer Scotland but they certainly penetrated it, and the results of their influence are noticeable in a chain of motte-and-bailey ruins. The Scottish mottes, like the mottes elsewhere, signify much more than mere fortification; they indicate that feudalism, with its law, its interdependence, and its land-holding pattern, had reached north Britain. Some writers refer to these mound castles as 'motes'. That they were fully equal to mottes elsewhere is obvious from such remains as Duffus, Elgin, Huntly in Aberdeenshire (from whose heights the Gordons were first able to make their proud claim to be 'Cocks of the North'), Urquhart on Loch Ness (better known perhaps for its alleged monster than its historical associations), and Bass of Inverurie (Aberdeenshire) where the motte may well have been about eighty feet high, thus ranking with the best in these islands.

Not all the influences are Norman. The Flemings were one of the most formidable peoples in the Middle Ages. They were as tough and forceful in their commercial dealings as they were in their military adventurings; a little too forceful in fact for the twelfth-century English, who complained so bitterly to Henry II of England that he banned them from his realm. They were welcomed in Scotland and before long were a considerable force in that land, particularly in Aberdeenshire. In their move north, and afterwards, they were accompanied by many other settlers, some English, some French. When times were good this was a happy

29   Bothwell castle. Never completed, it was nevertheless a magnificent castle. Note the donjon on the left of the picture; half of it was thrown into the Clyde by the Scots in 1336

arrangement, but when disaster struck the reaction of the Scots, whether soldiers or traders, was to blame and attack their immigrant neighbours; this situation is familiar to new-comers over many centuries and in many lands.

But the great days of castle-building – which means building in stone – were, as may have been expected, in the thirteenth century. The finest of these Scottish castles is generally reckoned to be Bothwell. Among its more striking features is a huge tower. This, in its day, resembled the great tower of Coucy, in north-east France, destroyed by the German army in 1917. (Regrettable though this was, the Germans could scarcely be blamed for denying such a useful observation post to their opponents.) Kildrummy has a similar tower, and it is not surprising to find this when we know that it was built in the reign of Alexander II, who was married to Marie de Coucy. It is believed that James of St George, already mentioned in connection with the Welsh castles, built the gatehouse at Kildrummy; he certainly built the one at Linlithgow. If so, this merely serves to illustrate the fact that there was nothing narrowly nationalistic about castles at the time; a castle was a castle whether in Scotland or Scandinavia, in Italy or Portugal, in England or Spain, and in most cases they looked alike.

During the Scottish wars of the first half of the fourteenth century, few castles were built, but instead there was a proliferation of tower-houses on both sides of the border. These were easy to construct, simple to command, and yet extremely formidable. It has been said that a tower-house was like a Saxon hall stood on end, putting the kitchens at the base, having the hall in the middle, and giving the lord's private apartments the dominant position at the top. The courtyard was enclosed by a wall known as a barmkin. Such towers became known as 'peels' or 'peles' from the Latin *palus* = a stake, derived through old French as 'pel'. As may be imagined, some were much more elaborate than others, but even the simplest form was adequate for local needs. The walls, which at first were solid throughout, were later hollowed out to provide an abundance of semi-private chambers. In the later stages the towers were built in the shape of a right angle with the main door in the inner part. When the Scots were no longer united against an English attack they gave much of their time and energy to fighting each other. Mercenaries were frequently used in these private quarrels and doubt about their loyalty and temper made it a matter of simple discretion to keep them apart, sometimes on the lowest floor, at other times in an entirely separate

30 Lochleven castle, fourteenth century: a five-storey tower house. The entrance, on the second floor, can only be reached by ladder. Mary Queen of Scots was imprisoned here in 1567

building. However, in all fairness it should be remembered that in some castles the mercenaries remained faithful to their paymaster when everyone else had given up the struggle; this had happened at Bridgnorth in 1101.

Doctor W. Douglas Simpson gives some impressive figures about the tower-house at Borthwick in Midlothian. He says: 'This majestic castle is executed with a beauty of masonry and richness of design unsurpassed in any like structure in the British Isles. It is entirely built of stone, vaulted in all its height, and the stone-slabbed roof rests directly on the uppermost vaults. The weight of this tower has been computed at not less than 20,000 tons; of this, 12,000 tons are accounted for by the ashlar work with which all the surfaces, inside and out, are cased.'[1]

One of the greatest problems of a castle-holder in Scotland was to guard it against a surprise attack. There are numerous stories of daring and unorthodox ventures against castles, and many of them were successful. As Froissart puts it:

> The Scottish men are right hardy and sore travailling in harness and in wars. They take with them no purveyance of bread nor wine, for their usage and soberness is such in time of war that they will pass on the journey a great long time with flesh half-sodden, without bread, and drink of the river water without wine and they neither care for pots and pans, for they seethe the beasts in their own skins.

Two hundred of these dour characters captured Edinburgh castle in 1341 by an ingenious stratagem, of which Sir William Douglas was the master-mind. Ten of the party, including Sir William and a few of his aristocratic friends, disguised themselves to look like poor merchants and with a load of meal, oats, and coal, carried on sorry nags, appeared at the castle gateway very early in the morning. The porter was in somewhat of a dilemma, for he did not like to rouse the

[1] W. Douglas Simpson, *Scottish Castles*, HMSO.

steward too early but on the other hand he did not wish to turn away goods that were so cheap that they might well find a market elsewhere before the castle staff was stirring. He therefore told them to come in and wait. As the Scots passed through the open doorway they overturned their load of coal so that the gates could not be closed, put a sword through the porter, and blew the signal call to the reinforcements hidden without. The ensuing bloody conflict may easily be imagined. Raids like this caused maximum destruction in minimum time but rarely altered the strategic situation, for the raiders usually retired within twenty-four hours carrying away everything they could not kill or burn.

Ireland, which did not see castles till the twelfth century, was no less of a problem to invaders than Wales and Scotland had been. The original inhabitants were the Ernai, a stocky dark-haired people who lived by hunting and fishing, and were placid in disposition. Later they were joined by tall, red-haired, blue-eyed people who seem to have originated from the German forests. They were tattooed and painted (in Scotland they were the painted men – the Picts), were gamblers, and loved hunting and horseback sports. They lived in a matriarchal society, and were well organized. Later came the Gaels, who were a branch of the Celts.

To the disciplined Normans these people must at first have seemed an easy prey, but few invaders can have been so rudely shocked. The Irish did not attempt to hold strategic positions; their tactics, if such a word can be applied to their rather simple way of fighting, was to harass, ambush, cut-off, and intimidate. There was no shortage of earthworks if they had wished to defend positions, for in the ninth century large areas of Ireland had been settled by the Norsemen, who had made formidable earthwork defences at strategic centres. In the early stages the Normans preferred to take hostages rather than leave small garrisons who might be wiped out and who could ill be spared from the main force. Although lazy to the point of fine art, the Irish were given to displaying much energy when it came to avoiding being a hostage. The latter's position was far from enviable. He was liable to lose his eyes – as happened at Exeter in 1068 – or his ears if it was thought that sending them to his family would have a favourable influence on negotiations, or he might quite simply be killed because he no longer served a useful purpose. Hostages always had to be men of influence and power; no one would care in the least if a peasant lost his eyes or his ears. Men of power and prestige were therefore necessary, and they would use all their influence to avoid being selected for that unattractive post.

As the Normans forced their way into Ireland they began to build castles. Hugh de Lacy raised a motte at Trim (Meath) in 1170 and left Hugh Tyrell as its Warden. Nearby, at Slane, there was soon another. Within a few years John de Courcy was building castles in Ulster, of which he became Justiciar in 1189. It is worth taking a look at this man for he typifies that desperate and enthusiastic fighting spirit which enabled the Normans to leave their mark from Scotland to Sicily, and across to the castles of the Middle East.

His family had settled at Stoke Courcy in Somerset, England, and he was said to be tall, fair, big-boned, and immensely strong and daring. He was always in the thickest of any fighting which came his way, but when not carving a path with an axe he was sober-minded, pious and modest. On a number of occasions he appeared to have taken one risk too many, but skill and luck got him out of trouble. His worst enemies eventually came from his friends, for when out of favour with King John he contrived to make an opponent of the powerful Hugh de Lacy. The latter captured him by treachery but he was eventually released from prison to fight a duel as the champion of England against the champion of France. But even after a period of prison diet de Courcy was still a fighter of such reputation that the Frenchman refused to meet him when he heard who his opponent was.

De Courcy was then put on show to demonstrate his strength, and ultimately was awarded his freedom. His former lordships in Ireland were restored to him and he set sail to claim them. Unfortunately for him, the weather was so bad that his attempts to land failed fifteen times, and as this appeared to be the will of Providence he returned to France to die.

Trim did not long remain a simple wooden tower on a motte. By 1220 it was a formidable stone rectangle with a square tower protruding from each of its four sides; a style which created a structure with twenty sides from which offence and defence could be maintained. An almost similar keep may be observed at Warkworth, Northumberland, the difference being that the wall towers are octagonal not rectangular.

Such castles had many functions other than defence. As administrative headquarters they granted and defined land areas, created manors, established villas, which later grew into towns, built mills, gave charters, introduced improvements in agriculture, and established commercial usage of rivers where formerly they had been mere highways for raiders. From all these they collected revenue, mainly in the form of fines. Soon the stage had been set for the great abuse of the absentee landlord, the man who could live comfortably off fines paid by peasants working on land which in all probability he rarely visited and might, in fact, never have seen.

But the Irish, no more than the English, the Welsh or the Scots, did not take these matters placidly. Orpen gives an interesting example.

'In 1257 Goffraigh O'Donell razed the castle of Caol-uisce, burned the town of Sligo, and in a fight at Credon in which he was sorely wounded routed a pursuing body of English.' The next year he was lying on his death-bed from these same wounds. 'But though O'Donell's body was stricken unto death his spirit was unbroken. Borne on a bier at the head of his men he defeated the Cinel Owen on the banks of the Swilley, and soon afterwards died the death of a hero who had at all times triumphed over his enemies.'

Friction between the English and the Irish had begun when Henry II of England decided to make his youngest son, John, King of Ireland. John resented the appointment, made when he would much rather have been off on a Crusade and in contact with more sophisticated amusements than the Irish countryside could offer. His policy towards Ireland was simply to give away large tracts of land to his friends in areas where they could not be held against local rebellion. Among the beneficiaries was Philip de Braose. Subsequently he had cause to regret any favours he had conferred on Braose, and in 1210 was actively trying to capture him. As we have already seen, the Braoses had an unfortunate penchant for upsetting those who might otherwise have benefited them. However, when John was King of England he proved to be an astute administrator, and in two months of the year 1210 he did more to settle and conciliate the Irish than anyone else before or since. Unfortunately he could not and probably would not have wished to stay to consolidate his reforms, and Ireland was soon back in chaos again. In consequence, the motte and bailey castles of the conquest were soon being replaced or supplemented by strong stone fortifications in a strategic chain with some form of local logistical support. There was a short interval of tranquillity in the next reign when William Marshal governed the country, and matters were tolerable until the reign of Edward II.

After their victory over the English at Bannockburn in 1314 the Scots decided to make gains in Ireland. As part of this policy Edward Bruce, brother of Robert, was sent with an invasion army and by 1316 had won enough victories to have himself crowned King. Unfortunately for Ireland, the only lasting effect of this move was the ensuing chaos. Bruce's allies fell out between themselves, and the English were able to slaughter the Scottish army and kill Bruce at Dundalk in 1318; the architect of victory was John de Bermingham, who took his name from the then small and unimportant Warwickshire manor. In the course of their campaign the Scottish army had marauded through the heart of the country, causing havoc and disruption. Quarrels between the Irish led to further destruction. When the country was subsequently being 'pacified', Edward had to retain a large following of Irish Kerns (Irish foot-soldiers) and necessity dictated that these had to draw some part of their support from the countryside they occupied – with no questions asked. Some of the English troops became more Irish than the local people themselves, and had to be restrained by law from adopting Irish habits. Among the prohibited practices was that of wearing the 'culon' – a long piece of hair which grew from the back and was pulled forward over the eyes masking the identity of the owner. It seems that human hair, which was unequalled for stringing balistas and weapons which worked by torsion and tension, has considerable power in arousing human passion and indignation. The fact that the Anglo-Normans were usually Welsh or Flemish meant that all too easily they adopted the habits of the country in which they had settled, whose way of life they usually found preferable to that of their patrons, the English.

In spite of deteriorating conditions in the later medieval years, castles exercised an increasingly important function in stabilizing the country and fostering trade. Even in 1295, the height of the Edwardian wars, Anglo-Irish trade covered such varied commodities as corn, horses, cattle, hides, salt meat, bacon, fresh salmon, lampreys, goats, pigs, wool, salt, cloth, silk, samite (a form of rich silk woven with six threads), gold, wine, iron, lead, tin, alum, cheese, butter, flour, and wood. Ireland's main exports were wool, leather, food, and wood, the last being in great demand for the construction of brattices around the battlements of castles.

It is always interesting to compare reputation with reality. As we have already seen, King John of England, for whom few have a good word, was one of the few men to do anything constructive and useful in Ireland. Unlike many other people he understood the Irish, their country and their needs. The universally loathed Piers Gaveston, favourite of Edward II and eventually murdered by Warwick, whom he had unwisely nicknamed the 'Black Dog of Arden', was also very successful in Ireland in 1308–9. He made a number of conquests and rebuilt, with great skill, a number of castles.

9

The People of Europe

With the advent of the Hohenstaufen dynasty in the first half of the twelfth century, Germany became a powerful force in European politics. Frederick I, nicknamed Barbarossa on account of his red beard, has already been mentioned in these pages. Barbarossa's path was not all roses for he spent the first thirty years of his reign in an internal struggle with Henry the Lion, who held the dukedoms of Bavaria and Saxony and was little less powerful than himself. As Holy Roman Emperor he had the care of certain Imperial territories in Italy and the consequent troubles took him across the Alps six times. Not least of his concerns were the Lombard cities. He destroyed Milan after a two-year siege, but it rose from its ashes and subsequently nearly destroyed him. His successor married the heiress to Sicily and Naples, which were united under Norman rule; and, as he gave more attention to this area than he did to his own kingdom, unity did not flourish in Germany. When this Emperor died, Innocent III had just become Pope (1198). He, of course, was the driving force behind the Third Crusade, but this was only one of his accomplishments. He founded the Inquisition, fought and beat Philip II of France, extended papal authority generally, and launched an attack on the dangerous Albigensian heretics. Ecclesiastics like Innocent III caused the medieval church to be regarded not only with respect but sometimes with awe and fear. The only king who did not regard his censure with apprehension was King John of England, a man who was not only impious but also proud of it, and prepared to brazen it out.

Frederick II, who became Holy Emperor very much at the instigation of Innocent III, was a worthy man who held the post for thirty years but rarely thought of his German territory, which he only once visited. In consequence, Germany was torn by internal squabbles and virtually ceased to exist as an entity. It was never the same again, although the first Habsburg, Rudolf, was elected Emperor in 1273, and Habsburgs succeeded to the Imperial crown for nearly six hundred years. The name Habsburg means 'hawk's castle', and refers to their home in Swabia, later Switzerland.

The effects of these near-anarchical conditions in twelfth- and thirteenth-century central Europe may easily be imagined. German cities went their own way, made their own provision for defence and their own arrangements for trade. Commerce developed briskly, and to safeguard trade along the rivers there grew up a profusion of castles, the ruins of many of which may be seen along the Rhine today. It was said, and probably rightly, there was a castle to every square mile in western Germany. But the greatest strength of Germany was probably its powerful commercial drive, to which all but a very few of the community contributed.

Travellers in Germany today will notice that castles are of every variety, and include large numbers of simple fortifications such as watch-towers. In mountainous country,

31 The castle as an observation point: this castle on the Rhine belonged to the counts of Nassau

castles have to follow the lie of the land and cannot adhere too closely to a set pattern. Defence therefore tends to rely on having plenty of small simple castles of moderate strength rather than large, allegedly impregnable, fortifications.

One German technique of castle-building was very simple and extremely effective. Basically it consisted of building a wall around the summit of a suitable peak and establishing all necessary accommodation within this perimeter. The labour, the effort, the hardship, and the danger involved in transporting heavy building materials to 'eagle's nest' types of castles must have been enormous, but we are so accustomed to finding them in countries all over the world that the human, or perhaps inhuman, side of such activities is seldom considered. The loss of life from accident, injury or disease was probably very high indeed, but this would be unlikely to deter the taskmasters or to slow down the speed, provided replacements were available.

Another popular form of German castle was that built on a peninsula, which would then be cut off from the rest of the land by a moat. These, like the peak castles, could be made concentric by the simple process of adding another wall lower down the slope. Facing the main approach would be flanking towers. Many German castles were designed to have the main defensive point at the gatehouse, but there were others which preferred the central tower or donjon. Elz, on the Moselle, and Marksburg near Braubach-on-Rhine, have central towers; Schönburg, on the Rhine, has a high curtain-wall on the approach road.

The interiors differed from their English and French counterparts in that instead of having a large hall and small rooms grouped round it, they tended to have rooms more moderately sized. However, what they lacked in splendour they often made up for in grace and proportion. Needless to say, they were as comfortless as castle interiors elsewhere.

Castles in Germany, as elsewhere, tend to vary according to the part they were required to play. In the areas with the more settled history they have been considerably modified for residential purposes; but in frontier districts they never lost their sense of military priority. One of the more striking of the frontier castles is Burghausen in Upper Bavaria. It was designed to keep out the Turks, and with its thousand yards of frontage, containing no less than six smaller castles, it seemed well fitted for the task.

In a book of this length it is obviously impossible to consider more than a limited selection of the castles of Europe, which are said to number as many as one hundred thousand if we count all the mottes, watch-towers, and ruins. It is, however, equally impossible to classify them as typical of the countries in which they were built. Austria, Germany and Switzerland naturally have a predominance of mountain fortresses and watch-towers, but the most striking castle in Switzerland is Chillon, on Lake Geneva. Castles in adjoining countries, for example Belgium, Holland and France, often have similar characteristics, but the ultimate factor in castle design, whatever the area, was its function in relation to the terrain. Unfortunately, there have sometimes been so many social, economic, and even physical changes (from draining or road-building) that it is not always possible to make a proper appreciation of how well that function might have been performed.

With the Holy Roman Emperor a German, it was inevitable that German history should be closely linked with Italian, and much of the latter's development depended on the fortunes of the Papacy. Apart from the portion south of Rome, which formed the Kingdom of the Two Sicilies, of Norman persuasion, Italy was divided up into areas held or claimed by the Pope or the Holy Roman Emperor. Of this, the Emperor controlled most of the north and west.

The Pope, as head of the Church, had power and influence which are difficult to visualize today. Scepticism, as we know it, scarcely existed; there were heresies and controversies but no one doubted that God was the universal creator. The Church, as we have seen, could inspire organizations as powerful as the Templars, Hospitallers, and Teutonic Knights, but these represented but a fraction of its influence. All learning, education and art was in its province; universities, schools, monasteries and religious houses spread its teaching; it exerted considerable domination over economic developments in trade and agriculture; its social welfare extended well beyond the field of poor relief; and the conduct of everyday life, from birth and marriage to death, was completely pervaded by religious principles. Before long, the Church was the largest landowner, and with the reins of this and other economic power in its hands, could influence, and even control, governments.

It is hardly surprising that an organization of such size and power should, on occasion, suffer from the ills that beset empires and be in frequent danger of accomplishing its own downfall. Popes like Innocent III were so successful that his lesser successors had their heads turned by the prestige of the office. Inevitably there were declines, and as mentioned in the history of Château Gaillard, between 1309 and 1377 the Popes were so completely in French power that they were compelled to live as virtual prisoners at Avignon. But this was the Pope in chains, not religion.

Unfortunately for its people, the one area of Europe most vulnerable to the rise and fall of Papal prestige was Italy. After the disaster of the 'Babylonian captivity' the office never recovered its former dignity and strength. In the absence of its spiritual leader Italy took its first step into the chaotic individualism that distinguished it until the nineteenth century. Recovery from the humiliation of imprisoned Popes might have been possible had not that disaster been followed by the even more serious one of the 'Great Schism', 1378–1471, when there were rival Popes, one at Rome and the other at Avignon, and a complementary host of rival bishops and Church officials.

The effect of weak government and the decay of authority is eventually to create a situation where man tries to fend for himself. Fortification is influenced by local conditions and resources. When the Normans made their conquests they paved their way with castles, which by the time of Edward I became the vast sophisticated buildings we have described. But in the rest of Europe, and particularly in Italy, less settled conditions obtained, and ambitions were commercial rather than political. Thus we find that although there is still a host of castles over Europe, there are also significant developments in the fortification of towns. Venice was one of the first to assert herself, and her merchants were able to finance a Crusade and use it to promote their own purely commercial ambitions (1204). Genoa and Pisa were on a scarcely smaller scale. In Lombardy there was formed a Lombard League which defeated the great Frederick Barbarossa. In Germany there were even more successful, or at least more enduring, combinations such as the Swabian, Rhenish, and Hanseatic Leagues, which last eventually commanded such vast economic resources that it was able to defeat the King of Denmark in 1362 after the latter's army had unwisely sacked one of the League's towns. One of the most romantic – to modern ears – of these associations was in Switzerland. At the time, this mountainous territory formed part of the district of Swabia; eventually it formed the 'Perpetual League' with the three cantons of Uri, Schwyz and Unterwalden. From this ultimately developed the State of Switzerland.

But medieval life produced two distinct types of person: there were those who liked to busy themselves in peacefully acquiring goods by trade, and those who found such an existence intolerable. The latter, who lived by armed robbery, eventually became such a nuisance that they were usually hired by one side or another to protect peaceful traders against itinerant freebooters. Mercenary forces have occurred throughout history but they can scarcely ever have had such rich pickings as when they were hired by the Italian townships of the later Middle Ages. Of all hired troops, the Condottieri were surely the most unproductive. Taking their name from their leader, who was called the Condottiere, they took entire charge of all disputes, which they then proceeded to settle with their own multi-national, almost entirely cavalry, forces. Discipline was severe but conflicts were virtually bloodless, on the understanding that everyone was in it for money; prisoners were more valuable than corpses, sides might be changed and forces realigned if the pay was right, and any aggressive feelings could always be vented on non-combatants. An exception to the general rule was the 'White Company', numbering about five thousand, which was formed after the Treaty of Brétigny in 1360 by Sir John Hawkswood; it stayed in existence for thirty years, fought honourably, and never went back on its word. But the rest of the Condottieri should not be regarded as being anything but a phenomenon among mercenaries. Many hired troops, notably the Swiss, fought with intensity and bitterness usually reserved for holders of fanatical beliefs.

Medieval Europe did not suffer from internal threats alone. In the thirteenth century there appeared yet another of those invasions from the east which had blighted whole continents in former centuries. On this occasion it was the Mongols, who raced across northern India, southern Russia, Persia and the Middle East, to Jerusalem. Fortunately Genghiz Khan's conquering army had virtually spent its force when it reached Europe, although Poland and Hungary experienced its power, speed and ruthlessness. Fortunately also, the organization of the Tartar hordes (horde = troop) was designed for conquering open plains, not mountainous, wooded, or marshy country. Even so, their efficiency was so great that even where they could not penetrate they were still feared. The army was composed of units in multiples of ten, and if one of any ten ran away or deserted to plunder, the remainder would be summarily tried and executed. A man's body should always be there to make up the number, dead or alive. The fact that these armies covered forty or fifty miles a day, were masters of every form of bluff and treachery, boiled down human captives to make incendiary fat with no more compunction that we should feel for animals used for the same purpose, and kept up a continuous attack night and day by operating a shift system, gave them a reputation for invincibility which was probably greater than they deserved. Unluckily for their opponents, the Mongol Tartars advanced over land which was ill-provided with castles. In consequence, they were able to concentrate their forces on the few fortified places there were, and starve, blandish, or batter them into defeat. As their lines of communication stretched over hundreds of miles, and their logistical plan was to live off the country they traversed, they were not usually in a position to undertake long sieges, although Sir Charles Oman instances an Alan fortress in the Caucasus which they are said to have besieged for twelve years. Their normal tactics of advancing in the shape of a crescent, of which the points, often out of sight at the beginning of an engagement, would fold swiftly inwards, surrounding the enemy and cutting him off from his supporters, were ideal for open plains like the steppes, but would have been thrown into disarray by a strategically sited line of fortresses. Large numbers would have checked them, but the areas they overran were too sparsely populated for an adequate defence force to be raised. Russia and Poland had plentiful timber but little stone; their feeble fortifications were soon burnt and overrun. Hungary was in a slightly better case. Trencsén held out against the invaders, and in consequence the following decades saw the erection of a number of square tower castles, of which Nagyvázsony, which still stands, is a good example. The Magyars, who were now settled in Hungary after a career much like the Mongols, massed enough numbers to make a fight of it but were eventually slaughtered at the Battle of Sajo; soon Hungary had followed the fate of southern Russia and Poland.

But once the Tartars reached mountainous country the picture was very different. Towns such as Olmutz and Brunn (now Olomouc and Brno), in Czechoslovakia, had fought behind their walls and been bypassed. And once the Mongols reached the mountains of Yugoslavia they were in serious trouble. They were drawn on, ambushed, cut off, or brought to battle in places where they could not employ horses or archery to any great advantage. The invincible hordes of the steppes were shown to be of very different mettle against prepared positions and fortified places. They themselves appeared to be the first to realize their own limitations, and in the middle of the thirteenth century fell back and were seen no more on this side of the Vistula.

The lesson was there for all to see. In previous eras barbarian hosts had been able to overrun vast tracts of country and to settle, enslave, or absorb the local people. The castle could put an end to all that, and had clearly demonstrated that great mobility might eventually be more of a drawback than an asset.

Before the West had seen the last of one invader another was rising in the East and preparing to launch a tide of devastation, slaughter and terror. It had always been so and presumably it would always be so. No one was surprised therefore to find that the Turks were even more persistent opponents than the Mongols; but it was a shock to find that they were more adaptable.

The Turks did not at first appear to be a more lasting force than any other of the conquering waves which had swept into the Middle East; time, however, showed they were to be infinitely more enduring. As we have already seen, the Seljukian Turks had overrun Syria, Armenia and Egypt, and twice just failed to capture Constantinople. Their advance alarmed the West and aroused what we might perhaps call its conscience; the result was the Crusades. But soon it was evident something far tougher and more permanent would be needed to stop the Turks, if they were to be stopped at all. By the end of the fourteenth century they had a reservoir of men of great fighting quality, an excellent organization, and leaders with a very wide experience of siege warfare. They had their own form of feudalism which conferred land on the basis that a man was *always* available for military service when needed. When a landholder died his estate was returned to the Sultan; his heirs would then receive a similar portion elsewhere. There was therefore no danger of a landowner developing too strong an association with his subject people and leading them in rebellion against their sovereign. And as the Turks were mostly polygamous and fertile, there was never any dearth of land-hungry sons prepared to help conquer new territories out of which bigger and better shares could be carved.

In addition, the Turks had an infantry contingent of unique quality; these were the Janissaries. Their recruitment was by removing the best boys, between the ages of seven and ten, from Christian villages which lay in Turkish territories. These children were then subjected to a ten-year period of training: minor disciplinary offences were corrected by flogging; more severe ones were dealt with by strangling. When their apprenticeship was finished they were the most dedicated, accurate, and skilled of infantrymen, equal to anyone in the use of the bow. And just as their early life had been influenced by severe punishment, their later life was sweetened by impressively generous rewards.

In spite of their efficiency and advantages the Turks did not have things all their own way; nevertheless, by the middle of the fifteenth century they were challenging the Byzantine, or Eastern Roman, Emperor. His capital, Constantinople, was the wonder of the Western world, and there was nothing remotely approaching it elsewhere. It was full of every form of magnificence from monasteries to palaces, markets full of the richest and most fascinating goods, and scholars and libraries with learning hardly guessed at elsewhere. Around the city were three walls in concentric pattern, and along them were numerous towers giving all the advantages of flanking fire. Nevertheless, in 1453 it fell to the Ottoman Turks, whose Sultan, Mahomet II, believed firmly in the value of artillery. It seems that he mustered a siege train of some seventy pieces, among them a monster which could project eight-hundred-pound balls. The remainder were capable of missiles of about four hundred pounds and seem to have been more reliable. Ten days of bombardment produced the first breach but a further month of steady hammering was needed before the Turks were able to get inside, so desperate was the fighting. Even then they were driven out again, their engines destroyed, and their mines filled in. Two more weeks elapsed, with the Turks battering the walls into rubble and trying here and there an escalade with ropes and ladders. But the very size of the city eventually brought its downfall. A small party of Turks crept in through a thinly-guarded postern; the effect on morale was devastating, as it so often seems to be on these occasions. Half a company of men who creep through into a rear area can cause widespread panic if there is no one nearby to rally a quick defence – and there seldom is, for all the leaders are up at the front. A cool and experienced man will weigh up the situation, assess the strength of the newcomers, and slaughter them as quickly as possible. But leaders of that calibre are seldom found in rear areas; in their absence, panic spreads and rumours abound. Constantinople was no exception. It was a repetition of the situation of 1204.

Curiously enough, there are very few cases of posterns causing the downfall of a citadel. Usually they are carefully watched, and are of course so designed to let people in or out one at a time. Their purpose is to enable a small force to slip out and take the enemy in the rear. A man standing on the inside of a postern should be in a position of overwhelming advantage over the person emerging from it, and should be able to kill him without difficulty in complete safety. But if discipline is relaxed for any reason, and a postern is unmanned, it is a different story. This particular postern, the Kerkoporta, had been used for sallies, but some careless soldier had forgotten to close it on his return.

The function of a castle, or even its style, does not always appear to have been affected by local conditions. Krak des Chevaliers, and many of the great Crusader castles, might just as well have been built in France or England as in the torrid mountains of the Middle East. Towers, of course, abound wherever there is mountainous country, whether in Scandinavia or Austria, the Rhineland or Switzerland, but they are also found in cities such as Bologna or Florence, each of which has over a hundred. Sometimes fortifications show signs of other architectural styles; the Zisa and the Cuba in Palermo are clearly influenced by Arab ideas. And often a castle will reflect the temperament of the people who built it. Norman towers were squat and square. What could

32   The castle of Loches, France, built in the twelfth century. The
donjon is 130 ft high, 80 ft long and 45 ft wide

be more foot-on-the-ground than Loches or even Angers?
In Spain, Perelada, Fuensaldaña and de Coca (a concentric
castle) defy the centuries with a pride which is impressive.

Spain's great achievement was Avila. It has a two-mile
wall of granite, with eighty-eight towers and nine main
gates, each of which is defended by flanking towers. It was
built by a mixed Jewish, Christian and Muslim labour force
between 1090 and 1099. There is no separate castle; the town

33　The Alcazar of Segovia, Spain, formerly the residence of the kings of Castille. Most of the superb interior was gutted by fire in 1862

is the castle. The earlier Spanish castles, and some of the later ones, had a central tower like the Norman donjon. This was where the castle-holder lived and was known, very appropriately, as the Tower of Homage. However, Spanish castles differed in one important characteristic from their Norman counterparts; they were not the private residences of feudal overlords but were barracks for garrisons. Feudalism never became established in Spain, thus the focal centre of a district was the town and not the castle. In consequence, Spanish castles had a different development from other European castles; they retained the donjon longer and did not introduce concentric design till many years after it had appeared elsewhere. These differences do not of course mean that they were in any way inferior to castles in other countries; they signify fulfilling a different function, which was the conquest and retention of Spain from the Arabs. Some of the early (twelfth to thirteenth century) castles had been built by the Orders of Knights which had been formed on the lines of the Hospitallers and Templars. Calatrava la Nueva, which was built by the Order of Calatrava in the early years of the thirteenth century was, and still is, one of the most impressive castles in Europe. Other military Orders, such as the Knights of Santiago, of Alcantara, of Montesa, and of San Jorge de Alfama, built and held powerful castles. Like all the Orders they grew rich and powerful and when their military requirement declined were accused of decadence.

Portugal, with many of the same problems as Spain, has numerous and similar castles. Many of them were built before the beginning of the thirteenth century and these naturally are of the donjon and bailey type. But one of the most interesting castles in Portugal dates from a much later period, the second half of the fourteenth century. This is

34   Lisbon castle. This fourteenth-century tower has been rebuilt.
Note the gunports

Amieira, which is a concentric castle with certain striking differences from the usual pattern. At each corner of the central court is a large square tower. The main entrance is under one of these towers, which is an Arab influence; the remainder of the design is closely linked with the Crusader pattern as it was eventually used in north-eastern Germany.

The earlier castles of France have already been described in the account of the development of motte and bailey

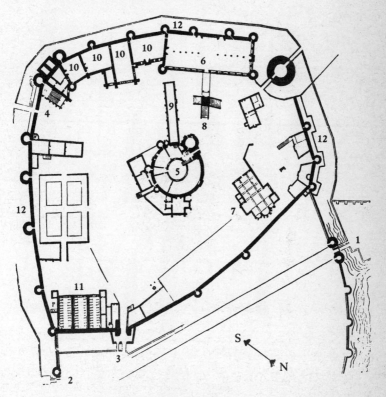

35 Plan of Montargis – a compact thirteenth-century French castle: 1 and 2, the outer gateways; 3, the inner gateway; 4, the postern; 5, the keep; 6, the great hall; 7, the chapel; 8, the staircase; 9, the gallery; 10, the barracks; 11, the stables and offices; 12, the moats

36   The donjon at Coucy. This could hold 1500 men. Everything –
doors, stairs, windows – were made large, as if for supermen

to stone structure. The Château Gaillard, with its round flanking towers and its stone machicolations, represented the ultimate that could be produced from this type of defensive concept. Montargis, early thirteenth century, which commanded the road from Paris to Orleans, is much more compact in design and makes greater use of flanking fire.

Dating from approximately the same period, probably 1220, the castle at Coucy had a donjon which, until it was destroyed in the First World War, was the most imposing and beautiful ever built (see figure 36). It could hold fifteen hundred men, and everything in it was made larger than was customary: seats, stairs, windows and doors were all made as if for supermen. In addition, the interior was decorated with ingenious colouring. It seems to have justified the boast of its owner, '*Roi ne suis, ne prince aussi. Je suis le Sire de Coucy*'. (Neither king nor prince am I. I am the lord of Coucy.) Coucy appears to have influenced not only Kildrummy in Scotland but also Landsee in the South Tyrol. Aigues-Mortes, by the Mediterranean, dates from 1240 and was used as the base for Louis IX's Crusade. It has a huge tower (the Tower of Constance) which is second only to Coucy. Angers has a multiplicity of closely-sited flanking towers along the curtain wall, which must have been one of the strongest ever built. They stand on rock which has been shaped to the line of the battered plinths at the foot of the towers and the wall.

But even in a country as rich in castles and medieval architecture as France the town of Carcassonne is outstanding. The town dates from Roman times, and has always been of great importance as it guards the highway from France to Spain. It was extensively repaired and strengthened in the latter half of the thirteenth century. A notable feature was the introduction of six towers with small prows running

down the front. Two of them flanked the Narbonne gate.
A curtain wall with further towers enclosed the other
buildings. This, where the slope of the ground permitted,
was further strengthened with a moat. There were also six
posterns which could only be reached from the outside by
ladders, a lesson that other castles and towns might have
profited by. Carcassonne has been so well preserved and
restored that it is still an authentic medieval town.

French influence is also to be seen in Switzerland, where
Chillon had originally belonged to the Counts of Savoy; in
Holland, where there were originally a number of mottes;
and in Belgium. Gravensteen at Ghent dates from 1180 and
has water defences, hanging towers, and good facilities for
flanking fire.

Scandinavian castles are not essentially different from those
in the rest of Europe. Kalmar in Sweden is virtually concentric with round towers. Although apparently relying on
passive rather than active defence it was regarded as the key
to Sweden. Gripsholm, dating from 1383, was redesigned
in 1537. Olofsberg, Finland, has interesting gun-loops. One
of the most impressive early castles in Denmark is Bastrop.
The reign of King Waldemar (1157–82) was the great period
for medieval military architecture in Denmark.

In Europe the castle, and its elder brother the walled town,
differed little, whatever the country. The only factor which
altered its appearance was the terrain. The presence of mottes,
or towers, or concentric or other designs of castles was due
to the fact that they were eminently suited to the military
requirement of the area. The Middle Ages did not build
'follies'. Such idiosyncrasies were reserved for the more
secure times of the nineteenth century.

10

Living in Castles

B ut how did men live in castles? Studies of medieval Europe frequently treat the Middle Ages as if they were an entity. But not only did century differ from century, but also there were areas of the continent where development was ahead of average and also places where it lagged far behind. Russia, of which a part must be regarded as Europe, had serfdom until the middle of the nineteenth century, and some countries have pockets which are medieval still.

To speak of the Middle Ages is to speak of one thousand years of history. For our purposes the period divides itself into two fairly equal phases: the first five hundred years, when Europe was forming itself into its component parts; the second, when stability was being produced by a system of castle and fortification. The latter period may be divided very roughly again century by century as the castle evolved. If we are to understand something of domestic life within castles we must examine them in each hundred-year period. Clearly, there is a vast difference between life in a wooden tower on a motte in 1051 and life in a building like the Sforza castle at Milan, after it had been rebuilt in 1450.

The first stage must obviously be life in the motte. Earlier in the book we gave a full account of the castle at Ardres, but there were probably few as elaborate as that. The majority of lords probably found it easier and more convenient to live on ground level on top of the motte; climbing and descending ladders is good for the figure but it is unlikely that the Norman castle-holders practised it much except when a castle was under attack.

There is an interesting contemporary account of a disaster which occurred at Merchem, which probably relates to the end of the eleventh century:

It chanced that in a town called Merchem Bishop John had a guest house. There was also close to the court of the church a strong place which might be regarded as a castle, or a municipiary very lofty, built after the fashion of the country by the lord of the town many years ago. For it was customary for the rich men and nobles of those parts, because their chief occupation is the carrying on of feuds and slaughters, in order that they may in this way be safe from enemies, and may have the greater power for either conquering their equals or keeping down their inferiors, to heap up a mound of earth as high as they were able, and to dig round it a broad, open, and deep ditch, and to girdle the whole upper edge of the mound instead of a wall, with a barrier of wooden planks, stoutly fixed together with numerous turrets set round. Within was constructed a house or rather citadel, commanding the whole, so that the gate of entry could only be approached by a bridge, which first springing from the counterscarp of the ditch, was gradually raised, as it advanced, supported by sets of piers, two, or even three, trussed on each side over convenient spans, crossing the ditch with a managed ascent so as to reach the upper level of the mound, landing at its edge on a level at the threshold of the gate.

In this retreat the bishop with his numerous and reverend retinue, after having confirmed a vast crowd of people both in the church and its court, by laying on of hands and the unction of the sacred chrism, returned to his lodging that he might change his vestments, because he had resolved to consecrate a cemetery for the burial of bodies of believers.

When in again descending from his lodging, in order to effect the proposed work, he halted. for some reason about the middle of the bridge which had there a height of thirty-five feet or more, the people pressing behind and before, and on each side, straightway the malice of the old enemy so contriving, the bridge yielded to the weight and fell shattered; and the crowd with the bishop fell to the bottom with a great crash of joists, beams, and planks, with great force and noise, while a thick dust enveloped the ruin so that scarce any one could see what had happened.

But though the eleventh-century castle-holder had strong enough fortresses he seldom spent much time in them. Much of his time would be spent trailing around the countryside after his king or, if his king did not require him, on various forays of his own. But his monarch did usually require him, and the accounts of eleventh-century Norman warfare astonish us by the amount of travelling it involved. William I collected his army for the invasion of England from all over Europe, and after the successful battle they were constantly on the move, to the Scottish and Welsh borders and back to Normandy. When we reflect that the trackways were far from good it seems unlikely that the King and his retinue could move, except in emergencies, more than twenty miles a day. Travel, even to the distant parts of England, would take three weeks if conditions were favourable, if the party did not have to dally, and there were no divergences. But matters were seldom as simple and straightforward as that. The Norman soldier, whether knight or infantryman, spent most of his life on the move.

Home-life in the castle was based on the hall. This showed little improvement on the Anglo-Saxon predecessor. The floor would be covered with rushes, dogs, scraps of food, bones, and dirt. Food was prepared and cooked out of doors; there was too much risk in having ovens in wooden buildings. Entertainment was no great problem; if a man belonged to the leisured classes he would hunt, drink, or tell witty stories to women; if he belonged to any other class (i.e. non-fighting) he had work to do, or, if he had not, he had the good sense to keep out of the way in case someone found him some. Drink exercised the function it has exercised since time immemorial.

The end of the eleventh century saw a general expansion of trade. Up till this time, commercial contacts between East and West had been tentative and limited; on one side of the 'iron curtain' lay the Arabs and the Russians, on the other the West. The Arabs had command of the Mediterranean from their bases in North Africa, from Spain and from the ports on the eastern shore; the Russians were too far away for anyone except the Scandinavians to be interested in trading with them. But suddenly the curtain was split. The Italians were the pioneers, and within half a century they were trading not only across the Mediterranean but also up the valleys of the Rhine and the Rhône. Wine, salt and wool made up the bulk but there were quantities of luxuries, of which spice was one of the more highly valued. Life in the eleventh- and twelfth-century castle was suddenly much enriched, but the most noticeable increase was in the consumption of wine. It was produced in ever-increasing quantities all over Europe, from Cyprus and Sicily to Burgundy and the Rhine, and whole fleets were employed in moving it around. England was a leading consumer. Much of the wine-producing area was in the English sphere of influence after Henry II of England married one of the great heiresses of all time, Eleanor of Aquitaine. This lady of dubious morals and erratic policies brought to the English crown a vast wine-producing area; her husband must have needed it. For three hundred years the wines of South-East France flowed without hindrance to England and, apart from some ale, was the main beverage. Not surprisingly, it was drunk in much greater quantities than it is today; nobody produced alarming figures about alcoholism, cirrhosis of the liver, or other unpleasantness, and there were no counter attractions such as tea, coffee or soft drinks. It was drunk by the bowl or hornful. Water was not popular; it was unsafe to drink even when mixed with wine, and too frequent bathing was thought to undermine the health. However, bath tubs existed: at Leeds Castle, Kent, there was a bathroom which enabled people to immerse themselves in the moat water.

Life was a blend of brutality and debauchery, but just as the former was occasionally tempered by a code of chivalry the latter was modified – one can scarcely say refined – by whims and fantasies. The court of William II of England and Normandy, which functioned between 1087 and 1100, was infamous for the extraordinary creatures who peopled it Most of them were homosexuals – or affected to be if they were not – and all wore fantastic costume such as long flowing robes (and hair to match) and shoes with points so long that they had to be tied by strings to the waist if the wearer was to walk at all. Yet there is no question that these affected perverts were exceedingly tough and enduring in the battlefield.

By the twelfth century, although there were numerous stone castles, mottes had not been entirely abandoned; however, the castle was beginning to take on much more of the shape of a permanent residence. The bigger baronial castles were as complex – perhaps more so – as the royal residences. They housed a variety of different peoples. There would be the administrators, which included the clerks, who saw to the profitable running of the estates. Next in importance, though not in numbers, would be the religious representatives; some of these would be administrators too.

The steward, who was originally the sty-ward (an important post when pigs were such a vital part of the commissariat), looked after a host of underlings. Among these were botilers or butlers (who saw to the storage and serving of wine), cooks, bakers, and scullions[1] (no shortage of jobs for them), chandlers for looking after candles, grooms, and a host of others. Not least of them was the ewer, for though it was not the custom to wash the body with any regularity it was essential – as already noted – to wash the hands before and after meals.

European castles were, for most of the year, cold, wet and murky. Damp and dark could not easily be countered in the absence of heating, but cold could be alleviated by clothing. As any old soldier knows, there is nothing more satisfactory for keeping out draughts than a blanket pulled round you; it may lack something in elegance but it is extremely efficient. Castle-dwellers wore their bed covers as garments. The wealthier people were able to have theirs lined with furs, of which ermine was a favourite, and remains a distinction of aristocracy today. Poorer people would be lucky if they had wool at all, let alone fur to line it with. More probably their draught excluder was of the same substance as their thread – nettles. The wealthier went to bed naked and the luckier ones had curtains around their four-posters. Poorer people wore their clothes day and night, and had little to put on their beds. In some castles the lord and lady had their bedrooms on the first floor, where they would sleep on a feather bed (in sharp contrast to the sleeping accommodation elsewhere, which consisted of benches at the best and floor at the worst). The room would have its own garderobe, and probably a stone washbasin much like the one which may be

---

[1] The word originally meant 'dirty fellow'; they were given the most menial tasks.

seen at Hampton Court, near Kingston-on-Thames, today.
The walls would be brightly painted, possibly with gold
paint, and decorated with striking designs. There would be
tapestries and other hangings. There might be a chair, of the
X pattern, and a cupboard or two. In summer there would
probably be a bowl of flowers, most likely roses.

The position of the lord was, in relation to his time,
enviable. Roger of Montgomery had almost the entire area
of Shropshire in his domain, not to mention huge estates in
other counties. A good portion of his staff's time was spent
in seeing that their feudal lord received his dues – and his
dues were many. He is said to have been entitled to 'droit du
seigneur', that is, the first night of the marriage with the
bride of any of his tenants, but the brides were probably too
numerous for the nights at his disposal, even if he were
interested. His lady might have had some influence in
restricting this due, for although women did not have many
rights in theory they appeared to exert a good number in
practice.

Lords grew rich because peasants worked for them without
being able to keep more than bare subsistence for themselves.
Apart from the work they had to do for the lord there were
endless irritating but unavoidable requirements. Corn had to
be ground at the lord's mill – for a fee; bread had to be baked
at the lord's bakery – for a fee; tillers and ploughmen had to
provide not only ploughs, oxen, and labour, but also seed
for the manorial land. As a plough-team consisted of eight
oxen – although they were not always yoked at one time –
cultivation was a major responsibility.

Law was everywhere in the feudal system, but this ensured
punishment rather than justice. If one man wronged another,
and this could be proved, the guilty man would be punished;
the injured man would have to extract what satisfaction he

could from the retribution inflicted on the wrongdoer, for there would be no benefits for the wronged.

The feature of medieval life which would seem more extraordinary today was the absence of privacy to which we have grown so accustomed that we forget that it is unknown in many parts of the world still, and would, in any case, be regarded as a dubious privilege. Castle life was community life; most people had seen their lords, and even their kings and queens, at close quarters, and many people had even touched them. Medieval men averaged about five feet five inches in height and women were a little shorter. Animals were also smaller, sheep being the size of large dogs today. When examining stairs, battlements, doorways and arrow-loops it is as well to remember these differences in size of the users, but though smaller they were not necessarily less strong, to judge by the seventy-pound pull required for a longbow.

Around the castle bailey, men would be doing a variety of jobs. John Smith, Faber, or Marshall, would be at work shoeing or working on armour, Tom Bowyer would be concerned with bows, Dick Fletcher with the arrows for them. Cooper would be busy with the casks which, when not storing liquid, would be used for cleaning chain mail, Hooper would be his partner; the rusty links would gleam like new after being rolled in a barrel full of sand. Armourers would be in close touch with Smiths, with Archers and Bowmen. Fuller would be cleaning cloth or preparing it for the dyer. Porter might be at the door, and be a man of some importance or sagacity, or he might be a simple dolt fit only for carrying other people's burdens, Salter would be important, although he would have more to do in France where there was a bigger manufacturing industry than in England. Labour was so plentiful that a man could have an amner or almoner to look after the cupboard, a biller to make axes, a bolter to sift meal, a fuster or foster to make saddle traces, a loriner or lorimer to make straps, a spencer to dispense. Some craftsmen exercised their skills on piece-work and their original description would be lost, as a souter (cobbler) might become a tasker, or a Gardner be called a Faraday because he worked for a day at a time; such 'journeymen' had independence but lacked status. If a man should have such extraordinary habits as to earn the title Drinkwater he would be ideally qualified for a post in the wine store (the boutierie or buttery).

All of them were socially superior to the wretched peasant whose labours kept them alive. The word 'villein' they applied to him did not originally imply he was anything but a downtrodden peasant, but as the years progressed, and as scapegoats often had to be found, the word began to imply an 'evil low-born fellow' – in fact a villain. Yet on this man's efforts the most elaborate feasts were based. J.J. Bagley in *Life in Medieval England* gives the figures for two such occasions, admittedly royal celebrations but probably not vastly different from those of the greater barons. He writes, 'During the Christmas festivities of 1246, Henry III's court ate, in addition to other food supplies, 5,000 chickens, 1100 partridges, hares and rabbits, 10,000 eels, 36 swans, 54 peacocks, and 90 boars; and when Richard II dined with his uncle John of Gaunt and the Bishop of Durham in 1387, they required 120 sheep, 16 oxen, 152 pigs, 210 geese, nearly 900 hens and capons, 50 swans, 1200 pigeons, quantities of rabbits and curlews, 11,000 eggs, 120 gallons of milk and 12 gallons of cream to satisfy the hunger of their combined retinues.'

Higher administration and crafts produced many names. Chancellors and Chamberlains looked after financial affairs and household management. Reeves were legal officers of some importance; when in charge of counties or shires they had great prestige; the shire-reeve is now familiar to one and all as the sheriff of cowboy westerns. A sheriff was also a chief magistrate of Mecca: *sherif* means lofty in Arabic. Stewards became increasingly important as the size of households increased. The title of Constable, on the other hand, seems to have fallen from its former greatness. At one time the Constable was the highest official at the French court; in England he was commander-in-chief of an area which might, if the King were overseas, be the entire country. The Constable's gate at Dover Castle, the gateway to England, gives an indication of his importance. However, in time some of these offices became hereditary, and families adopted the name in the later stages whether or not anyone was holding the actual office.

More, or Mather, doubtless owed his name to his skill at mowing and had the title bestowed on him by the Hayward, who stored the results of his labours in the castle stables as well as looking after all the fences and hedges (*haies*). Sower and Reaper would be in touch with Granger, whose province was the barn or grange – a word which now denotes much more than the original rough building. Food, whether for men or horses, provided the major quantity of names. Farrier, who was a veterinary surgeon as much as a shoesmith, was matched by Chaucer, who not only made shoes but also had ideas on chiropody. Leather gave scope for a variety of specialist trades; there were tanners and barkers, and listers who could dye either leather or cloth, and unusual skills such as that possessed by White-tawyer or Whittier, who dressed leather with alum instead of tanning and produced an attractive white material much favoured for gloves. Some of their occupations are obvious but others less so. Thrower would not easily be recognized as a silk-winder today, nor Harbisher as a maker of hauberks. Still less would Deathridge be recognized as a tinder-maker, although it derives from dyo-hryg; 'dyo' meant fuel and the original meaning of 'ridge' was to break up, as a field is broken up with ridge and furrow.

Verderers and Hunters, Hawkers, Falconers and Fishers were everywhere. Founders, who cast not only bells but also cannon, were not so plentiful. Nor were sporoners, who made spurs; perhaps they did not like to be confused with men who made spoons, or even 'spons', which were roofing shingles, and preferred the title Spurrier. But of course at any time these names could be swept on one side to describe a physical characteristic. Cruikshanks, Pauncefoot or Ponsford (fat guts), Vidler (wolf-face) or Coxhead (for a man who crowed too much). A trade might also acquire a nickname which would be less dignified than the original: Waghorn was a trumpeter, Knatchbull a butcher, Bevin a drinker, Hakluyt or Dolittle a lazy man, and Fettiplace an usher. But it would be an error to think that to give a dog a bad name meant to hang him. The Fettiplaces were distinguished lords who once lived in Appleton Manor, near Abingdon. Their tombs may be seen in Swinbrook Church, Oxfordshire.

However, surnames are not always a good guide to the nature or occupation of one's ancestors. Sometimes they are derived from place names, from the person who employed someone as a servant, or may even be chosen because they appeared to have a pleasing ring to them. This last holds true for most countries.

Although our predecessors were not particularly sophisticated in matters of hygiene they did at least have the sense to make adequate provision of garderobes or latrines. Some merely drained into the moat but others were much more ingenious than is popularly thought, and were about as efficient as a modern cesspool. Some of those on the ground floor are now mistaken for dungeons, and given the misleading title of 'oubliettes'. But castles were not prisons. A few captives had to be catered for, but it was not the custom to keep people manacled for long periods underground. There is an ingenious dungeon type of prison at Hastings Castle, Sussex. This was the first castle built by William the Conqueror on arriving in England. Half of its site and buildings have now disappeared, but the remaining portion which towers above the 'wrinkled sea' is enormously impressive. Under the old motte are caves with peculiar acoustic qualities. The lightest whisper travels a dozen yards, and legend has it that prisoners were put in the cellar and left alone. At the end of a curved passage, a dozen yards away, guards would stand listening and would hear every word – as it can be heard today. This phenomenon appears to derive from streaks of metal combined with unusual fluting in the rock.

By the thirteenth century life in a castle was far from spartan. Furniture was still minimal, but aumbries (cupboards) had been made in the walls, and there were plenty of chests for storing clothes and other goods. Crusaders and traders had brought tapestries and carpets back from the Middle East. Paint was always bright, and even the exterior of castles glittered in the sunlight. Glass was available but scarce. Some attempt was made to sweeten the atmosphere: herbs were strewn on the floor and occasionally lavender and other sweet-smelling seeds were left in bowls, as they still are at certain castles today, but more as tokens than necessities. Benches or forms were good enough, if not too good, for ordinary people but there were a few chairs for those worthy of them. The most important person at any meeting took the chair and by merely occupying that position indicated his authority.

Some of these buildings approximated in size and grandeur to what we now call a palace, a word which in those days meant little more than a hall, for which the French name was *palais,* the Italian *palazzo* (as today), and the German *palast* or *Pfalz.* A lord might have one or several residences; not every manorial region had a manor house but every baron had several large or small homes.

Land holding was extremely complicated by the thirteenth century, usually because it was intended to be so. Inheritance probably meant that a lord had a number of scattered domains but it was also the custom to confer land in small pieces spread over a wide area, and thus make it extremely difficult for a baron to assemble a rebellious force of his own tenants. As an example of the complications of land ownership there is the parish of Radway, Warwickshire, as described in Volume V of the *Victoria County History of Warwickshire*:

The hide held in 1086 by Richard the Forester descended as part of his serjeanty of Chesterton, and was held in 1198 by Hugh de Loges. His son Hugh alienated $\frac{1}{2}$ virgate to the Abbot of Stoneleigh and $7\frac{1}{2}$ virgates to Thomas, son of Richard Paveye, who enfeoffed Alan de Morcote. When Alan died he was said to hold 8 virgates in Radway of Thomas son of Richard 'of Warwick'; he left a son John then aged three. John may have granted some of his land to the Abbey of Stoneleigh in 1286 but at an enquiry held in 1298 it was stated that Hugh de Loges had alienated to Alan de Morcote 4 messuages and 4 virgates in Radway, of which Richard Payn was then holding 3 messuages and 3 virgates and John le Faukener the remainder; as these were parts of a serjeanty they were seized into the King's hand.

Such a tangled story is not at all unusual, and many areas were vastly more complicated.

Even in the fourteenth century there were still important castles made of wood. Durham was a wooden castle until 1343. Shrewsbury still had a wooden tower in the early part of the fourteenth century but there were probably stone buildings around it. A wooden tower could make an excellent look-out post and would be much cheaper and easier to erect than a stone building. Wooden buildings had a most serious drawback in that they were vulnerable to accidental fires. The curfew was an old custom which decreed that fires should be put out at a certain time. But not everyone goes to sleep the moment the light goes out and some people are prone to gossip unwisely, feeling that the dark is some form of protection. The reverse is, of course, the case, and would-be blackmailers crept around medieval villages listening under the broad eaves of the windows, where they could not be seen from above even on a moonlight night. But such eavesdroppers were recognized for the menace they were, so at the hour of 'cure-feu' it was not only a crime to have a light but also an offence to be on the streets at all.

Medieval life is usually assumed to have been unpleasant for all except the richest and most powerful. In comparison with modern material comforts this may well have been so, but there are still today people who are indifferent to comfort, and doubtless there were many more in the past. What, we might ask, made medieval man happy? Was he in fact less happy than the modern, who doubtless pities him? Life was undoubtedly shorter and a man was getting old at forty-five, but it was also more intense. And, of course, length of life seems to have depended on how lucky a man was in avoiding a number of illnesses which nowadays would not be fatal. In the castle there would be security and glamour; and, as labour was so plentiful, not too much work. There would be excitement, and entertainment, tournaments, quarrels, and an element of danger, but with it a highly satisfying feeling of belonging. This latter characteristic is well known to those who work in what they feel to be an essential position in famous institutions; they may stoke the boilers at famous schools, or companies, or establishments. They are part of the regiment, the ship's company, the aircrew. Others perhaps have more independence, but who cares: they belong.

And above all this they had a feeling which is sadly lost in our sceptical age. We know too much. They had the security that comes from knowing too little. Nobody went around creating endless alarmist news, to tell them they should ban the bomb, stop eating fats, avoid everything they had been accustomed to enjoy lest it should give them cancer, and finally crush all their idealism by telling them there was no future life. Nobody had invented the term 'do-gooder' to slander anyone who was prepared to raise his finger to help a fellow, or 'egghead' for a person who was concerned to think. Knowledge and learning were valued, and 'grammorous', the original of glamorous, which meant the ability to read and write, was highly esteemed.

Although some medieval writers complain bitterly, others appear to find that life was often full-blooded and enjoyable. Trevisa writes of fourteenth-century England:

> The erth of that land is copious of metal ore and salt welles; of quarers of marbel; of dyvers manors stones of red and white.

> Men behove to take hede of maydens; for they ben hote and tendre of complexion; smale, pliaunt and fayre of disposicion of body; shamfaste, ferdeful and merry touching the affeccion of the mind; they ben soon angry, and they ben mercyable and envyousse, bitter, gyleful, able to lerne . . . And for a woman is more meker than a man, she wepeth sooner, and is more envyousse, and more laughing and lovinge, and the malice of the soule is more in a woman than in a man.

We might be forgiven for asking plaintively what has happened to these entertaining hussies. They sound like a lost breed.

John Ball paints a sad picture of life as it was lived by the masses, in contrast to the pleasures enjoyed by the rich and privileged, but we might bear in mind that he was trying to stir his audience into action.

What have we deserved, or why should we be kept thus in servage. We be all come from one father and one mother, Adam and Eve. Whereby can they say or showe that they be greater lords than we be, saving by that which they cause us to win and labour for that they dispende? They are clothed in velvet and chamlet (soft leather) furred with grise, and we be vestured with pore clothe; they have their wynes, spyces and good bread, and we have the drawings out of chaffe and drink water. They dwell in fair houses, and we have the pain and travail, rain and wind in the fields. And by that which cometh of our labours, they kepe and maintain their estates. (Froissart's *Chronicles*)

Chaucer gives a more favourable view of the upper classes, among whom he spent most of his time. In the prologue to the *Canterbury Tales* he writes as follows:

> A knight ther was, and that a worthy man
> That fro the time that he first bigan
> To riden out, he loved chivalrye
> Trouthe and honour; freedom and courtesy
> Ful worthy was he in his lordes werre
> And thereto had he riden, no man ferre
> As wel in cristendom as in hethenesse
> And ever honoured for his worthynesse
> At Alisaundre[1] he was when it was won
> Ful oft time he hadde the bord bigonne[2]
> Aboven all nacions in Pruce [Prussia]
> In Lettow [Lithuania] had he reised [campaigned] and in
> Ruce [Russia]

[1] Alexander (Alexandria) was captured from the Turks in 1365 after a vigorous siege.
[2] Presided at a banquet.

No cristen man so oft of his degree
In Grenade at the siege eek hadde he be.

and so on:

At mortal batailles hadde he been fifteen
And foughten for our faith at Trasimene
In listes thries, and ay slain his foo.

It is clear that the knight is a battle-scarred veteran but no trace of pride or achievement shows in his bearing:

And though that he were worthy, he was wis
And of his part as meek as is a maid
He never yet no vileinge ne saide
In all his life unte no manner wight.
He was a very parfit gentle knight.

In this character description the knight represents an international ideal, like Parsifal, the hero of German chivalry; in real life the heroes may have fallen some way short.

His son seems a more realistic figure:

With him was his sone, a young squier
A lovyere and a lusty bachelor
With lockes crulle [curled] as they were leid in presse
Of twenty year of age he was, I gesse
Of his stature he was of even lengthe
And wonderly delivre and of greet strengthe
And he hadde been sometime in chivachye [cavalry skirmishes]
In Flaundres in Artois and Picardye
And born him weel, as of so litel space
In hope to standen in his lady grace
Embrouded was he, as it were a meede
Al ful of fresshe flowres white and reede
Singinge he was, or flutinge, al the daye
He was a fresh as is the month of May
Short was his gown with sleeves long and wyde
Wel coud he sit on hors and fair ride
He could songs make and wel endite
Just and eek dance, and weel purtreye and write

So hot he loved that by nightertale [at night]
He slept no more than doth a nightingale
Curteis he was, lowely and servisable
And carf [carved] beforn his father at the table.

In a survey of a field as broad as Europe, and over as long
a period as a thousand years, there will inevitably be considerable generalization. Yet curiously enough, progress
century by century is much the same from Lithuania to
Portugal and Denmark to Yugoslavia. Sometimes one
country will forge ahead of the others, or drop behind;
Spain was a hundred years behind England in adopting
concentric defence, but what English town could subsequently match Avila? As with design and discoveries
today, once they are made they seem to erupt everywhere.
The only people who have ever apparently managed to keep
a military secret to themselves were the Hittites; in 1500 BC
they discovered the process of smelting iron, and guarded
it for several centuries while they smote their adversaries far
and wide with their new swords. Fortunately for them, they
did not come into contact with some Danubian contemporaries who knew how to smelt but did not have
military ambitions.

Unfortunately, most medieval drawings give an unrealistic
impression of life as it was then lived. To the scholar they are a
rich mine of information but to the average man they appear
so simple, childlike and grotesque as to be hardly credible.
The characters scarcely seem human beings; the buildings
equally fanciful. Yet we possess today mementoes of
medieval skill which we could scarcely match. Great churches
like Durham, St George's Chapel, Windsor Castle, and
Westminster Abbey, and castles like Warwick, Caernarvon
and Dover could doubtless be reproduced, though it might
not be easy to do so. Certainly it would be an enormous

task if we had to build with only the facilities which were available for building at that time. Yet many people form their opinions of medieval achievement from drawings rather than cathedrals and castles.

It is, of course, ridiculous to assume that people who lived seven hundred years ago were as stupid as contemporary drawings made them appear, or that siege machinery was as crude as it is portrayed. We know that armour making was highly scientific and highly skilled yet believe that balistas and mangonels were strange and unwieldy constructions. The evidence of their efficiency and accuracy proves otherwise. Colonel E. Viollet-le-Duc, the eminent French military historian, had a brilliant grasp of the technique of siege warfare, yet his sketches are weirdly inefficient. Other drawings are worse. Some of the illustrations in books about medieval times were put in later editions by people who lacked the first knowledge of ballistics. The only drawings of siege machinery worth noting are those which appear in a book entitled *The Crossbow,* by Sir Ralph Payne-Gallwey, which first appeared in 1904. After a brilliant and lucid account of crossbows he turns to siege machines, some of which he constructed himself. These, it might be remembered, were the constructions of a man working on his own, using the equipment he might have had seven hundred years before. Presumably a king or powerful baron, hell-bent on reducing a fortress, would have had more resources and more experience than Sir Ralph. And yet we are expected to believe that they used implements which would have seemed crude to the pre-Christians.

In much the same way, many other medieval skills are discounted, among them medicine. Physicians of the time are said to have been unduly fond of blood-letting, and this may have been so, for monks, who probably had an austere diet, were bled three times a year in some monasteries. But for other people, who consumed vast quantities of wine and spicy food, it may well have been that the doctor knew what he was trying to achieve. Battlefields gave ample opportunity to study surgery. although dissection of dead bodies was forbidden by the Church. There are contemporary illus-trations of trepanning operations, and the advice given to surgeons was: drug or otherwise stun the patient, be as quick as possible over the operation, keep the patient warm afterwards, and let the wound heal from beneath rather than let it close itself too soon from above. Preventive medicine was also in force and men were told that if they wished to be healthy and live long they should eat sparingly, take plenty of exercise, and spend much time in the fresh air. There was undoubtedly a vast store of knowledge about the uses of herbs, which were not regarded, as so often they are today, as cranks' 'curealls' but as useful devices for regulating health. Many modern 'wonder drugs' were used in past centuries in cruder and less palatable forms, perhaps as moulds. Every woman would know them. Unfortunately, there would be in addition a selection of catchpenny drugs for the credulous. Poor old women who were not too scrupulous would produce love-philtres which had about as much beneficial effect as many heavily-advertised cosmetics today. But whereas witches might be ducked or burnt, cosmeticians and their copy-writers only grow rich.

The motto of our forbears might well have been 'waste not, want not'. The huge lavish provision for feasts, which we have mentioned earlier, would not be left unconsumed. Apart from those entitled to their share, every beggar and hanger-on for miles would appear. And when not feasting, the baronial household would have a plain diet. Even roses and violets, once they had bloomed in the castle garden, would disappear into the stew along with the mutton, onions and carrots. Many modern delicacies, such as fermented brews, mouldering cheeses, or over-ripe, and thus tender, meats were discovered by our forefathers because they had to be eaten bad or not, palatable or otherwise. The castle gardens, like the peasant's patch, would contain pears, apples, damsons and cherries, and these fruits would all be preserved if necessary in several different ways. In the fields crop yields were poor, being a mere four times the original, a fact which would amaze the modern farmer who is accustomed to five or ten times as much. Nor were animals very productive. Sheep were easier to rear than cattle, but sheep wool tended to be hairy and needed a lot of combing out, and the meat was not as plentiful as it would be on a modern animal. Sheep seem to have been prone to as many ailments then as now, from foot rot to scab, which was treated by applications of tar, thus giving rise to the saying, 'Don't spoil the sheep (not ship) for a ha'porth of tar'. Sheep's milk made an acceptable cheese, but this aspect of a sheep's productivity seems now to have become neglected.

Giraldus Cambrensis, who lived between 1147 and 1223, left us in *Itinerary through Wales* a description of the castle at Manorbier:

Manorbier near Pembroke is excellently well defended by turrets and bulwarks, and is situated on the summit of a hill extending on the western side towards the sea port, having on the northern and southern side a fine fish-pond under the walls, as conspicuous for its grand appearance as for the depth of its water, and a beautiful orchard on the same side, inclosed on one part by a vineyard, and on the other by a wood, remarkable for the projection of its rocks, and the height of its hazel trees. On the right hand of the promontory, between the castle and the church, near the site of a very large lake and mill, a rivulet of never-failing water flows through the valley, rendered sandy by the violence of the winds. Towards the west, the Severn sea, bending its course to Ireland, enters a hollow bay at some distance from the castle, and the southern rocks, if extended a little further to the north, would render it a most excellent harbour for shipping.

Gerald's pride would be shared by all the members of the castle staff. All were graded, and all honoured and feared the lord, but life was communal; they all ate together, descending

37   Castell Coch, near Cardiff, Wales. This somewhat unusual castle was completely rebuilt in the nineteenth century from plans of the thirteenth-century castle which once stood on the site. The 3rd Marquess of Bute who commissioned the restoration was an enthusiastic historian and archaeologist; he was also immensely rich

in rank as they sat away from the dais. Privacy and with-drawing rooms would come later and destroy the community feeling, but that was a long way off; for the moment, one could sit near enough to a king to hear him eat and drink.

A hundred years later the community was still intact but the extremes were greater, the grand were grander. In the twelfth century there was not much difference between the great and the not-so-great. They ate much the same, wore much the same, and thought much the same. But within a hundred years the grand would be enjoying more exotic foods, wearing richer and more elaborate garments, and have better arms, equipment and horses. By the time of Crécy (1346) a properly trained war-horse would cost £100, ten times the price of an ordinary steed. Their equivalent cost today would buy a Derby winner.

Much of the increase in elaboration was caused by monarchs. When Richard I set off on his Crusade he took fifty thousand horse-shoes with him, when Edward III set off on his French wars in 1360 he took not only horse-shoes but also mills, ovens, pavilions, six thousand carts, twenty-four thousand cart-horses, boiled-leather assault-boats capable of carrying three men, thirty falconers, sixty couples of hounds, and one hundred and twenty greyhounds. Needless to say his barons brought similar retinues, each trying to outdo the other.

Froissart gives an illuminating account of the year 1388, when Queen Isabel of France entered Paris to attend the celebrations which followed the signing of a peace treaty between England and France. Among the items he recorded are the following:

The great table of marble that always standeth still in the hall was made longer with a great plank board of oak four inches thick, which board was richly covered. And above the great table against one of the pillars was the king's dressing-board standing full of vessels of gold and silver, which was greatly coveted of many who saw it. Before the table along descending down there were barriers made of wood with three alleys, and there were sergeants and ushers a great number keeping the entries, to the intent that none should enter but such as were servitors of the table; for the hall was so full of people that a man could not turn him but with pain. Minstrels a great number pleasantly played, every man after his faculty. Then the King and the prelates and the queen and the ladies washed and sat down at the tables.

There follows a description of the King and Queen and their ladies-in-waiting, who were all dressed appropriately. He continues:

The press was so great that it was great pain to service them with their messes, which were great and notable. I have not to do to make great process thereof: I shall somewhat speak of the pastimes that were made between the messes, the which had been a great pleasure for the King to have seen if he had tarried out the whole dinner.

First in the midst of the palace there was a castle made of timber forty foot long and twenty broad, with four towers, in every quarter one, and one in the midst higher than the other . . . this castle went upon wheels, and which might be turned every way properly. This castle came to assault another sort . . . which also went on wheels so softly and covertly that the moving thereof could not be perceived. Also there was a ship properly devised wherein might well be a hundred men at arms, and all moved by the craft of wheels, both the castle, pavilion, and ship. They of the pavilion and of the ship assailed ever the castle, and they within the castle made great defence; but this sport endured not long, for the press of the people was so sore about them that no man could stir. The people were sore chafed with the heat and put to much pain. And there was a table by the partitioned chamber door, whereat sat many ladies and damosels, it was by reason of the press overthrown to the earth, and the ladies caused suddenly to rise without order, and sore chafed with the press and heat that was in the palace. The queen herself was at the point to have been sore displeased: perforce a back door was broken up to get fresh air. The lady of Coucy was sore dis-eased. When the King saw this matter he commanded to cease and the tables in great haste to be taken up to let the ladies and damosels at large; they left taking of wine and spices and went to their chambers.

All this happened at midday. At about five o'clock the Queen took part in a ceremonial procession through the streets. After that came supper, but the Queen had had enough. She stayed in her rooms.

The queen kept her chambers, she was no more seen that night. The other ladies and the king and the lords danced and revelled all that night, near hand till it was day in the morning; then every person departed and went to their lodgings to sleep, for it was time.

Not least of the remarkable features of this occasion was the display of presents from the burgesses:

First there were four pots of gold, six lavers of gold and six plates of gold, all this vessel weighed a hundred and fifty mark of gold. In like manner another sort of burgesses richly apparelled all in one livery came to the queen and presented her another litter, which was borne into her chamber – and sent her that present: which present was a ship of gold, two great flagons of gold, two dredge boxes of gold, two salts of gold, six pots of gold, six lavers of gold, twelve lamps of silver, two basons of silver; the sum was three hundred marks, what gold, what silver.

This by no means exhausts the lists of presents but gives a fair indication of the sort of wealth which could be produced on occasion.

Going to bed was by no means as simple a ceremony as it is nowadays. Servants had duties to perform, and did not neglect them, however irritating they might be to their masters. The bedrooms had to be warm, the feather bed smooth, and the coverings clean. The lord's clothes would be removed in a proper sequence. His nightcap would be put on and then his hair combed around it in appropriate fashion. Last of all the servant would drive out the dog and any other pets with sufficient severity to prevent their creeping in again the moment his back was turned.

Behaviour was most important. Children obviously needed instruction, but so did a large number of other people. Most of the precepts of medieval books would serve us in good stead nowadays. On entering the presence of your superiors you should greet everyone there but kneel to the lord. When spoken to, you should look the person who addresses you squarely in the eye, appear to be interested in what he is saying 'with blithe visage and diligent spirit'. Your reply should be brief and to the point. Stand till you are told to sit down, and then keep still. Do not scratch yourself or pick things up and fondle them. Do not speak unless you are spoken to. Do not make insolent comments on any unseemly behaviour by your lord, such as over-drinking.

Bread should not be broken, but cut with a knife. Don't lean over the table or stuff your mouth too full or drink when you are already chewing. Don't drop your meat in the salt-cellar but put a little on your trencher. And don't put your knife in your mouth.

These were ordinary requirements for decency. There were in addition a tremendous ritual and language for serving the meal itself. Meat was not just carved; it was partitioned according to certain titles. Deer was 'broken', goose was 'rered', swan was 'listed', hen was 'spoiled', peacocks were 'disfigured', salmon was 'chinned', trout was 'culponed', and so on, every meat having a different term for its dissection. The squire, a lad in his teens, would know all these terms and what is more how to portion such fowl as herons and cranes without making himself a laughing-stock or a source of annoyance. As some of them were baked in pastry, this was a task of no mean order. But squires performed it with grace that compelled widespread admiration. Sometimes his skill brought him amatory invitations which did not appeal to him but which he found difficult, if not dangerous, to refuse courteously and firmly. But anyone clever enough to carve thrushes and finches must expect to be considered a person of rare accomplishments and, possibly, unusual tastes.

Behind all the ceremony of feasting which, as we have seen, was by no means an everyday occurrence, there was a steady sequence of routine duties. The accounts for Chirk Castle, Denbigh, give an insight into the nature and scope of some of them. In the *History of Chirk Castle and Chirkland*, Margaret

38 Chirk castle, Denbigh, North Wales. The huge drum towers were designed to give protective fire to each other

Mahler quotes the accounts for 1329. They begin with repairs to watermills; these cost £3 2s. 0d. The figure should be seen against food prices, which in that year were one shilling for a sheep, and wheat 6 lbs for a penny. 1329 was a good year but plenty of memories went back to 1315 and 1316 when the rain had hardly ever stopped and there were no crops to reap. In those years, wheat, if you could get it and pay for it, would cost you 1s. 6d. a pound. Prices had never quite got back to the 1314 level but wages had risen, so nobody minded much.

The originals of these accounts are now in the Public Record Office. They deal with a variety of different outgoings:

Item the same renders account in payment of two carpenters for two gates to be made anew about the park of Chirk, and for paling of the said park at intervals round about each, to be repaired by the year 10s by view of Nicholas the forester and by tallage against the same.

And in carriage of timber for the said work 1s 8d.

Total 11s. 8d.

Item the same renders account in expense of the lord's wolf-hound and her eight puppies, the account beginning from the feast of St Michael to the feast of St Andrew the Apostle next following, 12s by tallage against Nicholas the Forester. And in expense of the aforesaid hound after delivering her puppies into the country, from the said feast of St Andrew the Apostle up to the feast of St Michael 10s by tallage against the aforesaid Nicholas.

Total 22s.

The expenses of sporting dogs and birds were liable to be higher than those for servants:

Item the same renders the account in expenses of 9 sparrow-hawks of the lord kept at Chirk after the taking of them, from Tuesday next before the feast of the Nativity of St John Baptist up to Tuesday next after the feast of St Mary Magdalene, for five weeks 3s by tallage against Nicholas the forester.

And in expense of two attendants carrying the said sparrow-hawks from Chirk to Bergeveny for 7 days going and returning 2s 8d by the same tallage.

And in chickens bought for them by the way 9d by the same tallage.

Total 6s 5d.

And in wages of the receiver for the same time to wit for the year £5. 6. 5½d taken by the day 3½d.

And in wages of the porter of the Castle for the same time 60s 10d taken by the day 2d.

And in wages of one park-keeper for the same time 30s 5d taken by the day 1d.

And in salary of one Chaplain for celebrating in the Castle for the year 53s 4d.[1]

And in salary of Howel ap Thomas interpreter of the lord in parts of Chirk 20s by the year.

Total £13 11s 6½d.

These of course are the accounts for a relatively new castle. In its present form Chirk dates from 1294 when it was begun, or 1310 when it was completed. The above accounts therefore fall within the first twenty years of its rebuilt existence. Previously it had been in Welsh ownership. Its twin – though not in appearance – is Dinas Bran, which overlooks Llangollen. Little remains of Dinas Bran, but no one who climbs the hill on which it stands is ever likely to forget it.

The first English holder of Chirk was Roger Mortimer, Justice of North Wales, but it did not stay with the Mortimers long, for his grandson sold it to the Fitzalans. It changed hands several times during the next one hundred and fifty years, and had a number of distinguished but not always fortunate owners. Eventually it was bought by Sir Thomas Myddleton in 1595. Sir Thomas was described as a 'merchant adventurer', which means that he made a number of successful expeditions to the Spanish Main. As he came of a family which traced its ancestry back to some notable early

---

[1] Mass was celebrated daily in castle chapels on first rising but was usually brief; everyone would attend.

warriors it was not surprising that he found no problems in an environment where not only the Spaniards were hostile. The Myddleton family hold Chirk still, the present owner being Lt.-Col. Ririd Myddleton, who served in the Coldstream Guards and commanded the 1st Armoured Battalion in Normandy in 1944.

The conquest of Wales and the building of the Edwardian fortresses was by no means the end of the military story for Wales. Like the Irish, the Welsh had a traditional system of land tenure and custom. In the year 1400, the Welsh people had little enough of their heritage left, but what they did have was regulated by a system which they could not understand and therefore hated. The only portions which could still be held under traditional Welsh law were portions which were so barren that no one could scrape a living off them. The inevitable consequence occurred when the Welsh again produced a great leader; this was Owen Glendower. In a matter of months he made himself master of Wales, and although his efforts eventually failed they were devastating enough at the time to make men wonder whether Wales might not be lost to England again. Naturally enough Chirk, commanding two main routes to Wales, was in the middle of the battle area and suffered accordingly.

For one year, 1462–3, Chirk belonged to Richard of Gloucester, later Richard III, the alleged murderer of the Princes in the Tower. The reason he held it for so short a time is somewhat of a mystery.

Today, Chirk is open to the public for much of the year. Although naturally somewhat different from what it was like in the days of its military glory as a border fortress, it nevertheless provides a better example of a functioning castle than the bare ruins in which visitors often try to imagine what medieval life must have been like. Castles were not always at war; some indeed never stood a siege at all. A castle which is lived in today may therefore convey something of the atmosphere of medieval fortresses which were thinly held for long periods when the countryside was peaceful and their lord was away on a campaign.

11

The Castle at Bay

The technique of siege was developed over many centuries and varied little from country to country. There were of course daring and unorthodox commanders, both in attack and defence, who would throw precedent to the winds and rely on shock or originality to achieve their aims. On more than one occasion the drawbridge was left down and the castle gates thrown wide open. The attacking force approached nervously, suspecting some trap, and were disconcerted to encounter a lively sally party which engaged them in open warfare outside the gates. Such flouting of orthodox principles proved too unnerving to the assailants, who had come prepared for a conventional leisurely siege, and they broke and fled.

The routine procedure for a siege was as follows:

The attack

1 Foment dissension in the surrounding district so that crops would be destroyed and potential opponents killed by each other.

2 Attract as many local supporters and traitors as possible, luring them by the promise of plunder.

3 Build a second motte a short distance from the castle under attack.

4 Set up siege engines within range of targets. Perriers and trebuchets were able to gauge range accurately by sliding the counterpoise along the beam; it was claimed that they were accurate enough to land a heavy stone on the point of a needle!

5 Set the miners digging trenches under the walls.

6 Fill in all ditches and moats, and bring siege towers up to the walls.

7 Create diversions while ladder parties try to scale walls.

8 Bring up battering rams and begin work on walls and gateways.

9 Aim stones from siege engines at points in wall which appear vulnerable.

10 Arrange for archers and slingers to sweep the battlements with continuous fire.

The defence

1 Call up all available manpower under 'castle-guard' duty and appoint look-outs.

2 Bring up crossbow quarrels, arrows, and other necessary materials from the stores.

3 Carry pitch, water, iron-bars and quicklime to the allure (rampart walk).

4 Sow all the castle approaches with caltraps (metal devices with four spikes, one of which would always be uppermost).

5 Construct engines for counter-artillery work.

6 Arrange frequent sorties.

7 Place mats in position to deaden the effect of battering rams.

8 Arrange ration scale, and, if necessary, eject non-combatants.

9 Have 'crow' ready. This was a hook on the end of a long pole by which unwary assailants could be snatched up. Subsequently they could be used for exchanges, or tortured for information.

10 Appoint listeners for counter-mining operation.

Froissart gives two interesting accounts of sieges, one of which was successful, the other not; the latter castle was well protected by water but also owed much to the courage and resource of its defenders.

The first siege was at Reole in 1345 during the first stage of the Hundred Years War:

Thus the earl of Derby came before the town of Reole and laid siege thereto on all sides and made bastides (small fortresses) in the fields and on the ways, so that no provision could enter the town, and nigh every day there was an assault. The siege endured a long space. And then the month was expired that they of Segur should give up their town, the earl sent thither and they of the town gave up and became under the obeisance of the king of England. . . . the Englishmen that had made in the mean space two belfries of great timber with three stages, every belfry on four great wheels, and the sides towards the town were covered with cure-boly (hides) to defend them from fire and from shot, and into every stage there was pointed an hundred archers. By strength of men these two belfries were brought to the walls of the town for they had so filled the dikes that they might be brought just to the walls. The archers in these stages shot so wholly together that none durst appear at their defence unless they were pavised [protected] by shields; and between these two belfries there were two hundred men with pick-axes to mine the walls, and so they brake through the walls.

The effect of this was to make the townspeople decide to surrender. However, like most towns, Reole had a castle adjoining it and the captain of the garrison decided to continue the battle from there: 'he went into the castle with his company of soldiers; and while they of the town were entreating, he conveyed out of the town a great quantity of wine and other provisions, and then closed the castle gates and said he would not yield up so soon.'

After some parleys, in which it became obvious that the castle would not surrender easily, the second siege began in earnest.

Then the earl entered the town and laid siege around the castle, as near as he might, and reared up all his engines, the which cast night and day against the walls but they did little hurt, the walls were so strong of hard stone; it was said that of old time it had been wrought by the hands of the Saracens, who made their works so strongly there is none such nowadays. When the earl saw he could do no good with his engines he caused them to cease; then he called to him his miners to the intent that they should make a mine under all the walls, which was not soon made. Eleven weeks later the castle was still holding out.

So long wrought the miners that at last they came under the base court but under the donjon they could not get for it stood on hard rock.

However, in the meantime, the miners had brought down a tower in the outer bailey. The defenders, not realizing that the donjon was defeating every effort of the miners and would continue to do so, decided the end was at hand and that they should ask for terms. This was a gentlemanly occasion, and terms were granted; the castle was surrendered and its occupants allowed to depart. On many similar occasions the end of the siege was the beginning of a bloody massacre.

Although medieval numbers are best treated with caution, and reduced by at least half, there must have been a considerable force engaged at Reole. Even so, it seems unlikely that each siege tower can have held three hundred archers. Still less does it seem remotely possible for the siege of Aiguillon, in 1346, to have been mounted with one hundred thousand men, as was claimed. Even Froissart appears to have doubts for he reduced the number to sixty thousand later; perhaps six thousand might be nearer the mark.

Aiguillon was approached across the river which, it was decided, must be bridged. However, the defenders produced three ships and crashed them into the bridge on which three hundred workmen were said to have been working day and night. The attackers then produced their own ships to defend the workmen who were then set to building again. Eventually the bridge was finished, but the attack over it failed and it was subsequently broken up by a group of defenders.

A new form of attack was now launched. The assault party was divided into four and each section took it in turn to maintain the attack for about four hours at a time. This went on for six days but still nothing important had been achieved. The besiegers then sent to Toulouse for 'eight great engines', and constructed four more on the site; all twelve began pounding the castle day and night. Much to their mortification the organizers of this stupendous battery found it achieved virtually nothing and had the further humiliation of seeing at least half their siege engines smashed to pieces by well-directed shots from inside the castle. Artillery was always liable to be caught by shots from inside the castle and was frequently attacked with 'Greek fire'.

The sallies from the castle were continuous and successful. On some of their forays the raiding parties captured most of the besiegers' stores. This vigorous harassing was in accordance with the classical technique of resisting a siege; never let the besiegers settle down and never cease to harry them.

Tremendous efforts, encouraged by the promise of large rewards, at length brought the attackers to the drawbridge, which they were finally able to drag down with hooks and chains. Alas for their efforts; they could get no further, had to retreat ignominiously, and had the mortification of seeing a new and stronger drawbridge replace the old one.

Fresh hope was kindled in the attackers when some master-carpenters offered to build extremely high scaffolding; this was to be brought up in ships and would enable the attackers to cross the walls at battlement level. Once again hopes were dashed, for the defenders had watched the development of this new threat and had built three siege engines, called martinets, to deal with them. The martinets made such havoc with the first scaffold that the attackers felt it would be a waste of good lives to risk men in the other three.

The only remaining weapon was starvation, but even this failed because before it could take effect the besiegers were called away for duty elsewhere. As a final insult, the defenders made a quick sally as the besiegers broke up, and took several prisoners.

The accounts of these two sieges exclude the daring individual deeds which could sometimes tip the scale between victory and defeat. A siege was full of temptation for both sides. An attacker wishing to distinguish himself, and earn a rich reward, might try scaling the walls by night, or would perhaps take a flying leap from an assault tower to the battlements. He might try his luck at dodging arrows and missiles until he reached a secluded corner from which it was difficult to dislodge him. Equally, there were great opportunities for the defenders. They could slip out of a postern and set alight a siege engine; returning to safety might be a problem but no one thought of such minor inconveniences at the time of setting out. Picketing was very poor, and after nightfall the opportunities for sabotage would be considerable.

There were however – as at Gaillard – sieges which departed from the convention of medieval warfare. When the stakes were high both sides became impatient and exhausted; as a result there would be provocative cruelty and retaliation.

Hostages would be hanged from the battlements, prisoners tied in sacks and thrown in the moat, and captives would be strapped in front of siege towers, where they could scarcely escape being killed by their own side.

Battle is an unpredictable business, and it is by no means certain that the best side will win. Mistakes are easily made, and can be disastrous. The difference between open warfare and siege was that in the former decisive errors were made on the day battle was joined; in the latter they were probably made when the castle was sited, designed, and built. Château Gaillard was said to have been too small to be impregnable, and there are many other castles in Europe with faulty design. Some have flanking towers whose field of fire is too restricted, such as that at Houdan (Seine-et-Oise), a twelfth-century castle; others have curtain walls which are too low or too extensive for their purpose. It should not be thought that all castles were perfect examples of fortification; some were merely a memorial to the incompetence of the architect and a death-trap to the defenders. It does not take an alert fighting-man long to spot a fatal weakness in an opponent's equipment, as tank crews and fighter pilots are only too well aware from experience in the present century.

12

The Mind of the Fighting Man

L ife in a castle in the Middle Ages had much in common with life in towns and villages. In fact, those whose home was the castle were more often than not to be found outside the perimeter rather than within. In the early part of our period the castle-dwellers had an almost complete monopoly of power and privilege. But money also represents power, and successful traders, who often lent money to kings at enormous rates of interest, had their share of influence too. Sometimes they overreached themselves and suffered, but for the most part rich traders knew they were safe; a king who defaulted on one debt was unlikely to obtain future assistance elsewhere, and the financial world has various subtle methods of putting pressure on those who incur its enmity. In the latter part of our period some traders and towns were immensely rich and could hire armies to defend themselves. The castle-dwellers therefore never had a monopoly of power except for very short periods, although power in some form or other was, in fact, exercised at all levels in the castle structure. Clearly the owner, the castellan, the constable, the officers and the soldiers were men whose word was law, but the varlets, the flunkeys and the workmen also exerted influence, partly as a result of reflected glory from those above them, and partly because there was credit from belonging to an impressive institution.

None the less the attitudes, however unrealistic, of people outside castles contributed considerably to the feelings of those inside. Regimental or unit pride is usually based on what a man thinks he ought to be rather than what he is. It lingers on after he leaves the Service and is often rationalized by a study of military history, but when he is actually serving he rarely feels any particular sense of history or duty but instinctively knows that the whole is greater than the sum of its component parts. But the castle represented greater stability than a regiment which moves around. It was a home. In fighting for it in a siege, a man, however poor, was protecting his own house. Perhaps it was set in the country-side he knew, and in which he might have been born. A regiment may advance, fall back, be linked to others; but a castle, although it might look a precarious one in wartime, was a home. As we have seen in the siege of Château Gaillard, when danger threatened the local people took shelter behind the castle walls. This use of a castle as a refuge was particularly frequent in border areas, where flocks would be driven into the bailey and the owners would man the walls. Different parts of the castle would be defended by different families, and in some fortresses a tower or piece of wall would be named after the family which provided 'castle-guard' for that particular sector.

It is of course customary to assume that life in the Middle Ages inside or outside the castle was uncomfortable and therefore unpleasant. We have seen that the reverse was true, that men took so little pleasure in physical comfort that they were constantly engaging in arduous physical activities, scourging or starving themselves, and engaging in campaigns which were ninety-nine per cent acute discomfort. Life in the medieval castle paid little attention to comfort because little store was set by it. Life for many by modern standards might be thought to have been utterly intolerable, but it could well be that the security and dullness and stability of modern life would have been as distasteful to the medieval lord as to the medieval peasant:

> Sound, sound the clarion, fill the fife
> To all the sensual world proclaim
> One crowded hour of glorious life
> Is worth an age without a name. (Mordaunt)

Commanders of castle garrisons faced problems which are all too familiar in the Services today. Most of them stemmed from boredom. To the outside world the castle would look immune to ordinary ills; to his staff, the commander would seem far removed from mortal cares. But, as every unit commander knows, the problems that face a commanding officer seldom vary and never cease. In wartime you know who is your enemy and which direction you can expect trouble to come from; in peacetime you may often feel that your friends and allies are a bigger nuisance than any enemy could ever be. But you never dare forget that the way you handle your troops in peacetime will ultimately determine the way they behave in wartime.

Boredom was no more and no less of a problem in the Middle Ages than it is today. Military life consists of short episodes of intense activity, usually accompanied by fear, and long periods of morale-destroying inaction which can have disastrous effects. Boredom will make men quarrel, raise silly complaints, gamble wildly and hate the person they lose to, become sour, and behave with dangerous recklessness. All these damage unit efficiency, and some may be fatal.

In hot countries bored garrisons may become infected with a form of hysteria. The effects always come as a surprise although the pattern is familiar enough. The atmosphere gradually begins to change from one of bored lethargy to one of suppressed tension. Even the air feels brittle. Chaff and banter go on in much the same way, one man talking too much perhaps, another too little. And then something snaps, and the man who has been unduly quiet is running amok or has set fire to the ration store, or has decided to walk home and is now three miles out in the desert with a sandstorm blowing up. The garrisons of Crusader castles must have been familiar with such irrationalities.

Medieval commanders used the time-honoured ways of keeping garrisons in fighting trim. They made them do weapon-training with bow, sword, axe or pick, they sent them on patrols, and they gave them building and repair work to do. They might, with discretion, make life in peacetime so strenuous that war would seem a pleasant rest. Veterans of the last two world wars will recall base 'rest' camps which were so full of petty restrictions and training requirements that return to the front was a holiday by comparison.

But in some respects castles created confidence and stimulated courage. Towering as they did over the landscape, they gave their occupants that understandable, but not always justified, feeling of superiority which human beings sometimes feel when they can look down on their fellow mortals. It is particularly noticeable when one person looks down on another from horseback. Defenders tended to treat their assailants with scorn and contempt. A wall which had been struck but not breached by a missile would be contemptuously wiped with a towel, and there were few jokes as good as that of covering a besieger with a load of stinking offal. Jeering would sometimes goad the attackers to reckless fury. At the siege of Chaluz (1199) arrows aimed at Gourdon were contemptuously deflected with a frying-pan.[1] Small wonder that when castles fell the victors often massacred the garrison with ill-tempered thoroughness. It has been said that no one can understand the mind of the medieval knight, and the implication is that his blend of arrogance, quick temper, risk-taking and irrationality is a thing of the past.

Curiously enough, the automobile has created its own species of knights. Lulled into a false sense of security by the armour around him, flattered by the speed which he controls with a touch of the foot, arrogant towards those with inferior mounts or with no mounts at all, the modern motorist will display chivalry towards an attractive woman, pay grudging deference to the owner of a vehicle which is clearly superior, but otherwise behave with stupid over-competitive hostility to every other road-user. The clearest conviction of the modern motorist is that every other driver is in the wrong; he is driving too fast, too slowly, too timidly or too aggressively. Even the carnage of the multiple accident leaves him relatively unmoved; the massacre of a few peasants had much the same effect on a feudal baron's emotions.

Like the medieval predecessor, the knight of the road goes into the lists and challenges all comers. This is the mêlée where he can work off his repressions and the ill-temper which everyday life engenders. Some drivers are worse than others but few of us have a completely unblotted escutcheon. Perhaps we are not so remote in thought from our distant ancestors as we like to believe.

[1] Chaluz, in Aquitaine, was being besieged by Richard I. Gourdon, a crossbowman, displayed himself flamboyantly. When Richard I, out of curiosity, wandered into range, Gourdon promptly shot him.

Conclusion: The Castle in Decline

Towards the end of the Middle Ages many castles were abandoned and neglected. This, as was subsequently proved, was a premature move, for the castle was to prove a formidable defence as late as the seventeenth century. However, fashions change in warfare as in other matters, and this would not be the last occasion when a military concept which had proved itself would be jettisoned for one that was merely a fashionable hypothesis.

The first reason for the decline of the castle was the weakening of feudalism; the second was the discovery of gunpowder. An essential feature of feudalism was that powerful barons maintained a decentralized government in which the principal figure was the king. Barons were men of great power, but for the most part they were held in check by other barons (who would support the king) and by the very considerable administrative responsibilities which their position gave them. As the king grew stronger the power of the barons grew less, and strong kings discouraged the building of powerful castles from which their unruly subjects might defy them. However, discouragement is one thing and complete prohibition another, so castles were still built but in far fewer numbers. They were less complicated and more compact than their predecessors, and had permanent garrisons of professional soldiers who brought their own problems and influenced the design in consequence. The lord of the castle could never be entirely sure of his hired troops so he took the precaution of living in a part of the castle where he was safe. That meant a gatehouse or a tower.

Among the more interesting of the later castles were Herstmonceux and Bodiam in Sussex, Caister in Norfolk, Tattershall in Lincolnshire, and Kirby Muxloe in Leicester-

39 Bodiam castle. Built in the late fourteenth century this was a simpler form of castle using an open court, without a central keep

shire. Herstmonceux (1441) and Bodiam (1385) were built as an insurance against the threat of a French invasion. Herstmonceux is built of brick and is more of an elaborate manor house than a rugged defensible castle. However, with its moat, machicolations, battlements, arrow-loops and gun-ports it is well equipped to give a good account of itself. Like its near neighbour Bodiam, it has mellowed with the centuries and is extremely beautiful. Internally, Herstmonceux is now simpler than first planned.

40   Herstmonceux castle. Built partly as a manor house but it was well-equipped to defend itself

Bodiam shows a return to a simpler plan than that of the Welsh castles built earlier in the same century. It has one central court, and therefore once the walls were breached a siege would be over. Nevertheless, this method was preferred to the complicated internal structures of some of the earlier castles which made movement so difficult for the defenders that they were unable to defend the outer walls effectively. Bodiam relied on strong corner and flanking towers firing over a wide moat. This design could be manned by a small force, unlike the more complicated castles which required large numbers of men. Curiously enough, this system of making the best use of inner, and therefore shorter, internal lines was soon to be overlooked by the great defensive architects of following centuries. We find engineers like Vauban, for example, making their buildings so complicated that internal mobility was restricted to the point where effective command became impossible.

Gunpowder was an innovation which for long had an influence it did not deserve. After a few striking demonstrations of its power as a terror weapon, its limitations were soon recognized; however, it lost neither prestige nor influence. The immediate deficiencies in attack were that it was slow and unreliable, and on more than one occasion unpredictable. In defence it was as likely to damage the structure of the building which housed it as the enemy strength. The effect was to encourage the building of partial fortresses, such as tower houses or fortified manor houses. Tower houses were usually adequate for local defence but fell some way short of being comfortable residences; manor houses were defensible and had the added advantage of being pleasant residences. Sometimes manor houses were built inside the remains of old castles which had fallen into disuse because they were too expensive to modify or man properly. The basis of this type of building was usually a low, sturdy building with battlements, a surrounding moat, and (probably) a tower. Once they became accepted as permanent dwellings they soon became as comfortable as the times allowed; in subsequent centuries they would be added to or modified and would successfully blend the architectural styles of several different periods. This type of building may be seen at its best in what are described as Bishop's palaces, as, for example, at Wells, England, or Lamphey, Wales.

One of the best known and most attractive of English fortified manor houses is that at Stokesay, Shropshire. It is called Stokesay castle, but is a house not a castle. The building was begun in 1240 but probably not finished till the end of the century. At that time it was surrounded by a curtain wall but this was reduced after it surrendered to the Parliamentarians in 1645. It has a five-sided tower, of which the two lower storeys were built in 1240, a long hall with a thirteenth-century hearth, and a solar – a withdrawing-room for the lord and lady.

The manor house is essentially an English development, but Continental influence on military architecture was very strong during the fourteenth century. This is evident at Caister (Norfolk), a brick castle with a high tower, which was clearly German inspired. Tattershall (Lincolnshire) could well have been built by the Order of the Teutonic Knights. It is really a tower-house and could be mistaken for a huge Norman keep; however, it was more of a residence than a fortress.

Other striking tower-houses may be seen at Raglan (Monmouthshire) and Ashby-de-la-Zouch (Leicestershire), both of which withstood formidable artillery bombardments during the English Civil War.

In simpler form tower-houses appear all over northern

England and Scotland. Threave (Galloway) is a typical example but there were numerous others, such as Warkworth (Northumberland), Belsay (Northumberland) and Yanwath (Westmorland). The Scots, like their English contemporaries on the other side of the border, were often at war with their neighbours as well as their traditional enemies. Survival required the maintenance of adequate defence but impregnable positions are rarely comfortable, so both sides had the dilemma of choosing between uncomfortable but secure towers and more comfortable but less defensible residences. Their military predicament was increased with the arrival of artillery. If a tower was tall it was more vulnerable to gunfire; if low, more susceptible to other forms of attack.

Unfortunately, one of the most interesting fifteenth-century buildings was never completed; this was Kirby Muxloe, near Leicester, in the English Midlands. Its owner, Lord Hastings, was beheaded by Richard III, who had a summary way with real or imagined enemies. Kirby Muxloe had a strong gatehouse and strong towers but its main feature was that it was designed to be defended by artillery against artillery. Like earlier castles it abounds with 'killing grounds'. It would undoubtedly have been a difficult castle to storm but its site can have been of little help to a potential defender.

The building accounts of Kirby Muxloe are available in full; it is interesting to note that the architect was John Couper, who built Eton College.

Although the great days of castle building ended in the Middle Ages, castles continued to be built in the following centuries and many of the ideas, good and bad, of the medieval architects continued to influence builders of fortifications. The ditch, for example, continued to appear long after it had ceased to have much practical use. Bastions and flanking fire, which had been developed in castle defence, continued to be used and perfected. The castle therefore was not a martial phenomenon, peculiar to its age, but a stage in the development of military building and skills. It was also, as we have seen, an important vehicle in the development of social and domestic life. It was, in short, one of the most extraordinary and versatile devices that man has ever produced.

Appendices

A CLOTH

Clothing and cloth were naturally of great importance in times when heating was extremely inefficient. Certain towns gave their names to materials which became well known. Thus we trace Worsted to Worstead in Norfolk, millinery to Milan, and jeans to Genoa.

All cloth was 'fulled' by being trampled on in water; the process both cleaned and thickened it. The people engaged in this process became known, and named, as 'fullers' or 'walkers'.

But before cloth could be woven the thread must be spun – a woman's constant task. Everywhere she went a woman carried the distaff, with a tangle of unspun threads at the end. It became a symbol of womanhood (compare spinster), and even queens were buried with distaffs in their tombs.

Clothing was much brighter and more multi-coloured than today. It was also an indicator of status; the more important a person was, the greater the length of his clothes. The belt also indicated status, hence the 'belted earl'. Some cloth lasted a long time but a man was despised by his servants if he was too careful with his clothes and made them last very long. Conversely, if he – or his wife – dressed too elaborately he might find himself burdened with duties he was not really able to afford.

B GIRALDUS CAMBRENSIS

Giraldus Cambrensis – Gerald of Wales – lived between 1147 and 1223 and faithfully chronicled the activities and ideas of his Welsh contemporaries. As the son of a Norman noble and the grandson of a Welsh princess, he was well qualified for his self-appointed task. In *Itinerary through Wales* he gives some illuminating facts.

In the twelfth century, Welsh arrows went through an oak door which was four fingers thick. Another Welsh arrow went through the armoured thigh of a Norman soldier and through the saddle into the horse; wheeling his horse round sharply, he was discomfited to be struck by another arrow which did precisely the same to the other leg.

Retribution for evil was much swifter in those days. At Winchcombe, near Cheltenham, there was a convent dedicated to St Kenelm.

On the vigil of the saint, when according to custom great multitudes of women resorted to the feast at Winchecumbe, the under butler of that convent committed fornication with one of them within the precincts of the monastery. This same man on the following day had the audacity to carry the psalter in the procession of the relics of the saints; and on his return to the choir, after the solemnity, the psalter stuck to his hands. Astonished and greatly confounded and at length calling to mind his crime on the preceding day he made confession and underwent penance; and being assisted by the prayers of the brotherhood, and having shown signs of sincere contrition, he was at length liberated from the miraculous bond.

Divine intervention seemed to him the only way of keeping the Welsh from their wicked ways, although it was not the only method which was tried. Henry 1 of England had imported a number of settlers from Flanders; however, the Welsh absorbed them.

Giraldus mentions an incident at Haverford which, he says, 'ought not to be admitted'. It certainly throws some light on medieval customs and philosophy.

A famous robber was fettered and confined in one of the castle towers (not, we note, below ground) and was often visited by three boys, the sons of the Earl of Clare, and two others, one of whom was son of the lord of the castle, and the other his grandson, sent thither for their education, and who applied to him for arrows with which he used to supply them. One day, at the request of the children, the robber, being brought from his dungeon, took advantage of the absence of the gaoler, closed the door, and shut himself up with the boys – nor did he cease, with an uplifted axe, to threaten the lives of the children, until indemnity and security were assured to him in the most ample manner.

A similar accident happened at Châteauroux in France. 'The lord of that place maintained in the castle a man whose eyes he had formerly put out, but who by long habit recollected the ways of the castle and the steps leading to the towers. Seizing an opportunity for revenge, and meditating the destruction of the youth, he fastened the inward doors of the castle, and took the only son and heir of the governor to the summit of a high tower from which he was seen with the utmost concern by the people beneath. The father of the boy hastened thither and, struck with terror, attempted by every possible means to procure the ransom of his son, but received for answer that this could not be effected but by the same mutilation of those lower parts which he had likewise inflicted upon him. The father, having in vain entreated mercy, at length assented, and caused a violent blow to be struck on his body; and the people around him cried out lamentably as if he had suffered mutilation. The blind man asked him where he felt the greatest pain. When he replied in his reins (loins), the other declared it was false and prepared to precipitate the boy. A second blow was given, and the lord of the castle assenting that the greatest pains were at his heart, the blind man expressing his disbelief, again carried the boy to the summit of the tower. The third time, however, the father, to save his son, really mutilated himself, and when he exclaimed that greatest pain was in his teeth: "It is true", said the blind man, "as a man who has had experience should be believed, and thou hast in part revenged my injuries. I shall meet death with more satisfaction, and thou shall neither beget any other son, nor receive comfort from this." Then precipitating himself and the boy from the summit of the tower, their limbs were broken, and both instantly expired'.

Giraldus gives a balanced account of Welsh military prowess:

They anxiously study the defence of their country and their liberty; for these they fight, for these they willingly sacrifice their lives; they esteem it a disgrace to die in bed, an honour to die on the field of battle . . . it is remarkable that this people, though unarmed, dares attack an armed foe . . . the horsemen as their situation or occasion requires, willingly serve as infantry, in attacking or retreating; and they either walk bare-footed, or make use of high shoes, roughly constructed with untanned leather . . .

In war this nation is very severe in the first attack, terrible by their clamour and looks filling the air with horrid shouts and the deep-toned clangour of very long trumpets. Bold in the first onset they cannot bear a repulse, being easily thrown into confusion as soon as they turn their backs; and they trust to flight for safety without attempting to rally. However: Though defeated and put to flight in one day, they are ready to resume the combat on the next, neither dejected by their loss, nor by their dishonour; and although they do not display great fortitude in open engagements and regular conflicts, yet they harass the enemy by ambuscades and nightly sallies.

Giraldus goes on to point out that the reason why the first three Norman kings had very little trouble with Wales was that the English almost exterminated the Welsh people just before the Norman Conquest.

C CASTLE OFFICIALS

Castle offices were usually hereditary and their holders took their names from their occupations. Hence words like

Steward (or Stuart) and Marshall appear frequently in national as well as local history. Any form of feudal service was called 'serjeantry', although a serjeant was originally a man who organized foot-soldiers. Some of these callings perhaps appeared more important then than now. The name 'Trist' or 'Trister' signified a huntsman, whose 'tryst' was his station. The assignment he organized would be with a fat buck rather than a buxom maiden.

The late J.H.Round wrote an interesting article in the *English Historical Review,* Vol. XXXIII (1920), in which he clears up several misconceptions about castle staff. He draws a clear distinction between the castle watchmen (the vigiles) and the castle guards. The former were paid by Waite fee. The function of waits as watchmen has long since been taken over by other bodies such as the civil police, but in some areas they still provide a band which plays for charity.

In general, castle staff fell into two groups. These were:
    a Military
    b Administrative

The military, as we have seen, were probably local knights doing their turn as castle guard. Most of the others would be permanent employees on scales of payment which varied considerably between castles. However, we note that in 1180 the pay of a knight was 6d. to 8d. a day while that of a chaplain at Rouen castle was 6d. a day, the same as the porter. On the other hand, the porter at Vaudreuil received only 2d. a day, which was the same as the ordinary watchmen. The porter at York, an important castle, was a serjeant who had an estate worth £5 a year as well as land in the town itself. Porters had to be men of quick suspicious minds if they were to survive. Medieval history is full of accounts of porters who were slain 'so privily'.

Chaplains had functions which extended well beyond the spiritual sphere. They were 'viewers', which meant that they were educated men of no special technical ability. Then, as now, there was the feeling that the technician might not see the wood for the trees, and that the best management comes from people with general rather than specialized education. Ingeniators (literally, 'clever fellows') handled the technical engineering side and were the expert clerks of the works; their pay was 7d. a day. Chaplains held positions of varying importance but were always highly esteemed. In the early Norman reigns the Chaplain looked after the King's treasure chest, which was kept in the King's chamber. He was therefore often called the Chamberlain, although the fact that he sat behind a screen known as the Cancella also gave him the name Chancellor. The word exchequer, which is usually associated with Chancellors nowadays, comes from the checked cloth by which illiterate sheriffs measured out their receipts and payments. The administration of Norman justice consisted of punishing the guilty, not compensating the wronged; it was therefore profitable to administer.

D ARMOUR

The manufacture, care, and use of armour was obviously of vast importance and occupied a large proportion of castle time and staff. The Normans arrived in England in 1066 with conical helmets, from the front of which a short bar known as the nasal jutted; a mail coat, or hauberk, which was covered with rows of iron rings; a long oval shield rather pointed at the base; a lance, a long double-edged sword, a mace (which was a form of club), and bows and arrows. In the opposing army they saw axes, but despised them; a hundred years later they were popular even with kings.

Armour, of course, does not wear out quickly, and obsolete but still serviceable Norman equipment could still be encountered on battlefields as late as the fourteenth century. (Chain mail captured from Crusaders is still worn for ceremonies in Northern Nigeria, where it was taken by Arab chiefs.)

However, by the end of the twelfth century most knights had abandoned the mailed shirt, and instead wore a short-sleeved knee-length tunic which was made of ring or chain mail and might be of double or triple thickness. This was pulled into the waist by a belt, and had a hood which could be drawn up over the head or hang down from the back of the neck as required. Underneath he would wear a tunic which would probably be quilted. His helmet would be iron and would fit closely. His long sword was supported by a cross strip over his left shoulder, like a modern Sam Browne belt.

Curiously enough, the changes that took place in armour seem to have been dictated more by fashion than military efficiency. Both sleeves and hauberk became longer, gauntlets of leather or iron came in, as did leggings (chausses) of chain mail and metal shoes known as champons. The belt dropped to the waist again.

In the thirteenth century the headpiece, or helm, became a massive cylinder which was flat on the top, had bar openings for vision and holes for breathing, and was so large that it almost reached down to the shoulders. This cumbrous device was worn by Crusaders in temperatures approaching 100° Fahrenheit.

So far the construction of armour had been fairly simple, but in the thirteenth century some care was taken to protect vital areas. Elbows, knees and armpits, all of which would be exposed by movement, were protected by small, carefully wrought pieces of iron. Then, as this seemed a profitable policy, metal plates were buckled over the other chain-mail surfaces, making breastplates, arm guards and greaves shaped to the leg. Even then men preserved a remarkable degree of agility, and the spectacle of an unhorsed knight lying helpless on his back like an overturned beetle did not occur till two centuries later. However, the development of what might have appeared to be a fully protective suit of armour did not make the knight abandon his shield; it was smaller and less

41 A statue of Gunther von Schwarzburg, King of the Romans, in
full armour, 1349

42   Brass of Sir Nicholas Dagworth, Blickling Norfolk, 1401

cumbersome than the former versions but it was still a weighty addition. When on horseback he usually carried it slung over his shoulder, but when charging to battle he wore it suspended by a strap from his neck; his right arm was therefore free to hold his lance or sword while his left could be used for signalling his commands.

By the end of the century both helmet and foot armour had become more pointed but the suit was beginning to become over heavy. However, the battlefield was a dangerous place to choose for removing one's helmet to mop one's brow; an observant longbowman was liable to make it one's last movement (as when Lord Dacre was shot by a boy in 1461 at Towton, in Yorkshire). The lance also added to the general weight; it was now too long to be thrown. The knight might have seemed invulnerable but the archer or foot-soldier who opposed him knew differently. Horses could be brought down with arrows or pikes, armour could be cracked with flails, helmets could be dislodged with slung stones, and daggers could penetrate chinks between plates. All this time, and for a century after, the sword was used for a cutting stroke, and never for thrusting or parrying as in fencing.

The experience of the Crusades, in which the Turks enjoyed greater mobility because their armour was lighter, might well have encouraged the Western knights to lighten their self-imposed load; but it did not. The revolution came from the mercenaries, who had to be progressive in their ideas if they were to live to draw another day's pay. They soon discarded the cumbersome helm and replaced it by a globular headpiece, pointed in front and on top, which was called the basinet. The neck was protected by a coif of mail which hung downwards. The face was completely covered by what the French called a mursail – from its resemblance to a dog's muzzle – but the English more politely called a vizor; however, the English did not always bother to wear one.

Swordsmanship developed slowly, but by the beginning of the fourteenth century there were weapons which could be used for thrusting as well as cutting.

In the fourteenth century the main development in armour lay in the way it was tailored to the figure. The long hauberk was shortened and the appearance of a knight at a short distance resembled that of a skinned rabbit. Appearance counted for little on the battlefield, but the absence of protection around the loins soon brought in a form of iron skirt, which, being made up of overlapping plates, gave protection without impeding mobility.

Evolution was not, of course, complete. The basinet was effective but was too constricting. It was therefore replaced in the fifteenth century by a helmet which spread out over the back of the neck and projected in a bowl shape at the front to protect the mouth and chin. This part was called the beavor; the word is sometimes used today as a slang description of beards. Below it were flat plates of metal jointed together to protect the throat. They were called gorgets; their replica is sometimes to be seen in the white cloth facings of some modern uniforms.

The ultimate development of armour falls outside our period, but two features should be noticed. Ceremonial armour became heavier, more elaborate and more decorated; working armour became lighter and more practical; the only significant improvement in design was the ridge which appeared between breast plate and cuirass, which, being carried out to a point, gave the appearance of a chicken's breast. But although mainly outmoded by the weapons and tactics of the seventeenth century, armour did not go out of use for another century. And today in Vietnam experiments are being made with bullet-proof vests, which are not popular because they weigh thirty pounds!

E ARTILLERY

Early artillery consisted, as we have seen previously, of a variety of weapons which worked by tension and torsion. Catapults or mangonels, working by tension, propelled darts or spears which would impale several men at a hundred yards or more. Balistas could fire arrows in precisely the same manner as a catapult or sling stones weighing up to five hundred pounds. Many of these projectiles carried incendiary material. More effective than either was the trebuchet, which worked with a counterpoise.

The exact date of the invention of gunpowder is not known, and it is probable that the discovery was a matter of evolution rather than the brain-child of one ingenious inventor. The first mention of cannon is in 1338 at Cambrai (firing darts and crossbow quarrels). Soon it was also discharging small (three-pound) balls of stone or lead. These had a great initial effect on morale but were soon recognized to be comparatively ineffective. There was an element of uncertainty about the use of these cannon which stemmed from the fact that they were made of bent plates held in iron rings and were not properly sealed at the back.

In a very short time, cannon had become enormous. They acquired a number of names, of which bombard was the most popular, and were soon so overloaded in proportion to their construction that they were often more dangerous to the gun-crew than the enemy; disasters were mainly due to the fact that their users hoped that they could throw the same weight as a balista or trebuchet. As the gunpowder was either slow-burning and ineffective, or fast burning and uncontrollable, the medieval artilleryman had an interesting dilemma. A further problem came from elevation and direction. Unless the cannon was firmly and laboriously fixed, its aim was most erratic, but the process of making a position safe from recoil might take more time than could be spared in a brisk engagement.

Some improvement in efficiency occurred when stone balls were hooped with iron. Experiments with case-shot and heated shot proved disastrous.

Even when the discovery of casting led to the introduction of bronze cannon there was still a considerable element of risk. Nobody knew the exact proportion for the copper and tin alloy, and nobody knew how to purify saltpetre consistently. However, in spite of a series of disasters, bronze cannon became steadily more effective. Gun carriages produced mobility, elevation was produced from curved side-supports, and the recoil was mastered by the use of trunnions.

The word 'shell' did not come into the military vocabulary till some time later: in the sixteenth century the Germans invented the mortar and called its projectiles 'shells'.

Early hand-guns displayed the same early weaknesses as cannon but were favoured by mercenaries. They were first seen in England when they were carried by Burgundian troops at the Second Battle of St Albans, in 1460. They fired lead pellets and feathered darts, but without much effect. Eleven years later, when Edward IV landed at Ravenspur, he brought with him three hundred Flemings armed with hand-guns. However, as these guns could only manage one shot per hour they put up a poor show against longbows, and were useful mainly as a reserve weapon and morale factor.

F APPEARANCE AND CLOTHING

The appearance of the people who are mentioned early in this book is largely a matter of conjecture. Records do exist – in mosaics, effigies and manuscripts – but these may well be misleading according to whether the artist wished to idealize or vilify the subject. One assumption which we can make without fear of being proved wrong is that the early warriors – and some of the later – all bore looks of unrelenting fierceness. The muscles of the face settle slowly to the expression worn by the owner when he is not concerned with the impression he gives. Thus a face that may be charming and ingratiating when a man wishes to please temporarily may well wear an entirely different aspect when he is not interested in the opinions of those around him.

Even when civilization had softened some of the brutalities of life, men – and often women – wore sombre expressions. One can but pity the jesters who had to work to amuse such moody audiences. Humour was, of course, crude and cruel. The word buffoon – a synonym for jester – is derived from *buffare* (to puff out the cheeks), a gesture likely to be the reaction to another's discomfiture. To arouse interest in those whose normal diversions included watching tortures and executions required an ingenious turn of mind.

Hair, and the way it is arranged, affects not only appearance but also demeanour. Customs varied among early European peoples, some tribes wearing beards while others were relatively clean-shaven. Long moustaches, often accompanied by long hair, were popular. Beards were disliked by the Huns, who are said to have had their cheeks slashed in childhood to prevent the growth of hair on the face. Beards never went out of favour completely in medieval times, partly perhaps because of the difficulty of shaving, and by 1500 were almost universal.

Women, being unable to grow beards and moustaches, compensated for the fact by greater variety in hair styles. Often they had long plaits which would have been suicidal for men to wear. Hair would be worn flat on the head and plaits stretched to full length by attaching weights. Plaited hair was usually released and flowed free when women were in private. It is said that when Matilda of Flanders was 'betrothed' without her consent to William I she was displeased and made a number of disparaging remarks about the appearance and parentage of her husband-to-be. William, learning of this, went swiftly to Lille where he found her in a sewing circle surrounded by her attendants. Grabbing a handful of her free-flowing hair, he dragged her around the floor by it, beat her with the other hand, and finally flung her on the ground at his feet. His courtship was successful. She gazed up at him with adoration and expressed her great enthusiasm to be his bride.

Fashion began to play an increasing part after the eleventh century. Austere peoples such as the Normans, who had won the Battle of Hastings short-haired and clean-shaven, were soon affecting the manners of the conquered; half-a-century later they wore a fringe over their foreheads and bobs of hair over each ear.

Excessively long hair was criticized in the later Middle Ages as being a mark of effeminacy, or at any event of a corrupt and licentious outlook damaging to military efficiency. This was a reversal from the Frankish attitude, for in that nation long hair had been a mark of nobility and hair of great length had distinguished people of royal birth. Side-whiskers, which had been a mark of adventurous young men in the Greece of 500 BC and a mark of respectable middle-aged conformity in nineteenth-century Europe, found little favour in medieval times.

At all times in history conditions of great luxury led to tasteless extravagance in fashion; the best phases occurred when life was settled but not too secure.

Women usually covered their heads with a piece of folded linen which was held in place by a metal circle. This became better known as the wimple, and a general idea of its appearance may be gained from the headgear of nuns today. There were of course numerous ways in which this head-covering could be folded to give variety.

Allowing for slight variations caused by changes in fashion, medieval women wore the following clothes:

The main garment was a tunic which fitted closely to the hips, reached almost to the floor, and was cut low at the neck to show the garment beneath. It was secured at the waist with a belt, often jewelled. Over this would probably be another fuller garment. Sleeves were sometimes gathered in at the wrists, but at other periods were flared outwards. Tunics and belts were fastened with pins or buckles, which could be elaborately jewelled. Men also used buckles or clasps. For greater warmth there would be a fur-lined cloak; for greater display there would be an over-tunic heavily brocaded. By the fourteenth and fifteenth century many European women possessed an impressive collection of garments which included such materials as velvet, damask, sarsenet (a very soft silk), satin and mink. Fortunately for their husbands, most of these materials were very hard-wearing and would last most of a lifetime. Then as now, people often dressed more elaborately than their status required and their finances justified. Headgear developed from the wimple to the capuchon, or chaperon, a tall hood which remained in favour till the late sixteenth century.

Many of the words used for clothing today originated with Anglo-Saxon or Norman-French words. 'Froc' was Norman-French for a coarse cloth. Short under-tunics were given the name sherte' or 'sceort' in Anglo-Saxon, while the French called them 'camises'. 'Braccos' were a form of loose-fitting drawers which ultimately developed into breeches. 'Soccas' were short hose, and the Anglo-Saxon 'gunna' had already acquired the form 'gown' in French. Under-garments were usually of spun hemp, linen or wool.

Women quickly became aware that pins could be adapted to other uses than holding together their clothes, and as a result there was soon legislation restricting the length of these semi-lethal weapons. Then as now, women were prepared to suffer in the cause of beauty. They would weigh themselves down with cumbersome headdresses or heavy clothing or ornaments, cover their skin with powder made from crushed grain, and even pluck out hair in order to create the impression of having a high forehead.

Men's clothing was less elaborate than that of women but not necessarily less ornate. Under active service conditions men tended to wear similar clothes, short tunics, leather jerkins, cross-gartered hose. Armour was not, of course, everyday dress, and a jerkin of boiled leather was often tough enough to turn a sword-cut.

Later it was possible to distinguish rank not only by the richness but also by the length of clothing. Nobles would wear robes reaching to the ankle, merchants to the calf, and peasants to their knees. These were known as 'cottes'. Surcoats would be lined with fur of varying quality.

G RECREATION AND THE MEDIEVAL MIND

Anyone wishing to know the appearance of a medieval hall should visit the dining halls of Oxford or Cambridge; there it may be seen today complete with benches, minstrels' galleries, and screens. The floor covering is different; and oil paintings now hang where a medieval owner would have had tapestries. Harpers and minstrels have departed from the galleries, and the screens – wooden partitions – are no longer necessary to hide the sweating cooks from the diners.

In the solar – the room opening off the dais – there would be scope for diversion. Perhaps there would be a parrot or two, for the Crusaders had introduced these noisy pets; a game of chess, which had been known since the eleventh century; backgammon and cards. The latter did not possess their modern appearance but distinguished the suits by a variety of symbols such as bells, roses, acorns and leaves. Gambling with dice and cards was so widespread and rash that there had been legislation attempting to regulate it in the Crusaders' armies.

Animals and birds, ranging from lapdogs and monkeys to hawks and larks, would be regarded as toys by young and old. Kites, windmills and other models would amuse all ages and classes.

Much of the fascination of medieval Europe lies in its contrasts and incongruities. Men lived and fought in castles on land, so they built miniature castles on ships, the forecastle and sterncastle, although it was soon apparent that such designs had a strictly limited application and terrifying liabilities. We recall the cumbersome helmets of the Crusaders, and cannot but marvel at the endurance of a man who could not only wear armour in the tropics but keep it on for days on end and fight with great energy when he might well have been dropping with exhaustion. We recall that extraordinary character, Edward IV of England. By the age of nineteen he had already proved himself a successful general and a skilled politician, but long before he died at the age of forty-one he had ruined himself physically and mentally by intemperance in everything. Although his wife had borne him ten children he had numerous mistresses, and his endurance at drinking and feasting were beyond the capacity of any of his contemporaries. The man who had killed his horse at Towton (1461) and fought dismounted all day in a snowstorm, in one of the bitterest and bloodiest battles of history, was also a self-indulgent fop. During his reign, dress became more absurd than it had been at any time since the reign of William Rufus, and he himself was always in the forefront of fashion. Perhaps the principal difference between medieval and modern man is that today he is less disposed to these violent extremes.

Glossary

Allure	The wall-walk behind the battlements.
Ashlar	Squared stone blocks used for facing.
Bailey	Enclosure around the castle, also known as the 'ward'.
Balista, *or ballista* (*Latin,* onager)	An engine for propelling stones.
Barbican	A defensive outwork, usually in front of the main gate.
Bar sinister	Bar on left of shield, sometimes denoted illegitimacy of wearer.
Bastion	A defensive projection. Sometimes it was a circular tower but more sophisticated versions had two faces and two flanks, making, with the rear wall, a pentagon of irregular sides.
Belfry	Siege tower.
Bombard	An early cannon with a range of several hundred yards.
Braie	Low defensive platform which impeded attacks on lower walls.
Brattices or hoards	Wooden platforms built out from the battlements. Slots in the floors enabled the defenders to fire on those immediately below.
Casemates	Galleries built outside the base of the castle walls with apertures through which archers could fire into the faces of battering-ram parties.
Cat	Bore or ram.
Catapult	Siege engine which fired large darts. It was a large and powerful weapon but worked on the same principle as its modern counterpart.

Chausses	Protective mail on the legs.
Crenellations	Battlements. The stone part, known as the merlon, was usually pierced with a cruciform arrow-loop; the open part was called the embrasure, or crenelle, and was sometimes covered with a wooden shutter.
Curtain, *or chemise:*	The wall around the bailey.
Donjon	Originally, the tower; when gatehouses replaced donjons, these towers were used as prisons; the word donjon or dungeon described a prison long after it had ceased to be a part of the tower.
Escutcheon	Shield with armorial bearings.
Espringal	Another word for a siege engine.
Gambeson	Quilted tunic worn underneath the hauberk.
Garderobe	Latrine.
Hauberk	Coat of chain mail.
Hide	One hundred and twenty acres approx., but varied in different parts.
Juliet	Circular donjon.
Keep	Donjon. The word 'keep' was applied to donjons in later centuries but was not used in medieval times.
Machicolation	Brattices built of stone.
Mangonel	Siege engine for slinging medium-sized stones.
Solar	Withdrawing room (away from main hall).
Trebuchet	Siege engine which worked by counterpoise. It was one of the few weapons to be invented in the Middle Ages: the majority were copied from earlier times.
Virgate	Thirty acres (one-quarter of a hide).

Select Bibliography

Arbman, H., *The Vikings*, Thames and Hudson, London/Praeger, New York, 1961.

Bagley, J.J., *Life in Medieval England*, Batsford, London/British Book Service, New York, 1960.

Bark, William C., *Origins of the Medieval World*, Oxford UP/Stanford UP, 1958.

Bradford, E.D.S., *The Great Betrayal*, Hodder and Stoughton, London, 1967.

Chenevix Trench, C.P., *The Poacher and the Squire*, Longmans, London, 1967.

Coulton, G.G., *Medieval Panorama*, Cambridge UP/Macmillan, New York, 1945.

Crosland, J., *William the Marshal*, Peter Owen, London/Copp, New York, 1962.

Hassall, W.O., *How They Lived*, Blackwell, Oxford/Oxford UP, New Jersey, 1962.

Kavli, Guthorm, *Norwegian Architecture*, Batsford, London and New York, 1959.

Lewis, M.A., *Ancestors: A Personal Exploration into the Past*, Hodder and Stoughton, London, 1966.

Oman, C.W.C. (revised and edited by J.H. Beeler), *The Art of War in the Middle Ages*, Oxford UP/Cornell UP, 1960.

Partington, J.R., *History of Greek Fire and Gunpowder*, Heffer, Cambridge/Barnes and Noble, New York, 1960.

Pullan, B.S., *Sources for the History of Medieval Europe*, Blackwell, Oxford/Barnes and Noble, New York, 1966.

Sayles, G.O., *The Medieval Foundations of England* (2nd edn), Methuen, 1950.

Simons, E.N., *The Reign of Edward IV*, Muller, London/Barnes and Noble, New York, 1966.

Tomkeieff, O.G., *Life in Norman England*, Batsford, London/Putnam, New York, 1966.

Toy, S., *Castles of Great Britain*, Heinemann, London/British Book Centre, New York, 1953.

Toy, S., *A History of Fortification (3000 BC to AD 1700)*, Heinemann, London/Macmillan, New York, 1955.

Turner, E.S., *The Court of St James*, Michael Joseph, London/St Martins

Press, New York, 1959.

Tuulse, A., *Castles of the Western World*, Thames and Hudson, London/Longmans, New York, 1958.

Wallace-Hadrill, J. M. (ed.), *Fredergarii chronicon: Fourth Book of the Chronicle of Fredegar*, Nelson, London/Oxford UP, New Jersey, 1960.

Weissmüller, A. A., *Castles from the Heart of Spain*, Barrie and Rockliff, London/Potter, New York, 1967.

Whitelock, D. (ed.), *The Anglo-Saxon Chronicle*, Eyre and Spottiswoode, London/Rutgers, New York, 1962.

The following titles are now available only from libraries, but are nevertheless of great interest and usefulness.

Armitage, E. S., *Early Norman Castles*, 1912.

Boutell, C., *Arms and Armour*, 1893.

Cambrensis, G., *Itinerary through Wales*, 1908.

Clark, G. T., *Medieval Military Architecture*, 1884.

Cleophan, R. C., *The Tournament*, 1919.

Corroyer, E., *L'Architecture Gothique*, 1891.

Deville, A., *Histoire du Château Gaillard et du siège qu'il soutint contre Philippe Auguste en 1203 et 1204*, 1849.

Foulks, W. D., *Paul the Deacon's History of the Lombards*, 1907.

Gibbon, Edward (edited by J. B. Bury), *Decline and Fall of the Roman Empire*, 1898.

Grose, Francis, *Military Antiquities*, 1786.

Harvey, A., *The Castles and Walled Towers of England*, 1911.

Hewitt, J., *Ancient Armour and Weapons in Europe*, 1860.

James, M. R., *De Nugis Curialium of Walter Map*.

Mackay Mackenzie, W., *The Medieval Castle in Scotland*, 1927.

Mahler, M., *Chirk Castle and Chirk Land*, 1912.

Meyrick, C. R., *A Critical Enquiry into Ancient Armour*, 1824.

Morris, J. E., *The Welsh Wars of Edward I*, 1901.

Orpen, G., *Ireland under the Normans*, 1911.

Round, J. H., *Feudal England*, 1895.

Round, J. H., *The Staff of a Castle in the Twelfth Century*, 1920.

Sargeant, Lewis, *The Franks*, 1898.

Viollet-le-Duc, E., *Military Architecture of the Middle Ages*, 1860.

Viollet-le-Duc, E., *Annals of a Fortress*, 1875.

Watson, J., *Memoirs of the Ancient Earls of Warren and Surrey*, 1782.

Index